The X Factors

*Exceptional Financial Strategies
for Extraordinary Times*

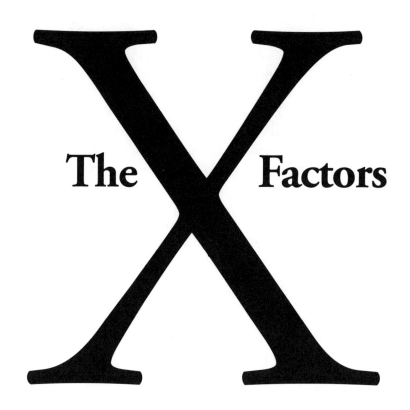

The X Factors

*Exceptional Financial Strategies
for Extraordinary Times*

JERRY WHITE

with Frank Condron

Warwick Publishing

The X-Factors:
Exceptional Financial Strategies for Extraordinary Times
Copyright ©2005 by Jerry White

We acknowledge the financial support of the Government of Canada through the Book Publishing Industry Development Program for our publishing activities.

ISBN: 1-894622-54-5

Published by Warwick Publishing Inc.
161 Frederick Street, Suite 200
Toronto, Ontario M5A 4P3 Canada
www.warwickgp.com

Distributed in Canada by
Canadian Book Network
c/o Georgetown Terminal Warehouses
34 Armstrong Avenue
Georgetown, Ontario L7G 4R9
www.canadianbooknetwork.com

Printed and bound in Canada

Contents

SECTION A

The X-Factors

What Are the X-Factors?

The X-Factors are exceptional strategies for extraordinary times.

Regardless of age or level of investment experience, all investors can benefit by learning new and innovative ways to take control of their financial futures by taking charge of their personal finances, and the X-Factors can help investors do just that.

This multi-part program is designed to educate you in personal finance strategies for the coming decades. Why? Because things have changed. The world of personal finance is evolving every day, and strategies that worked fifteen, ten, and even five years ago are not necessarily applicable to the current investment environment.

The X-Factors truly are exceptional strategies for extraordinary times—the times we are living in right now, and the times to come. These strategies focus on the present and the future, because it is only future wealth that counts. The past investment mistakes you've made and past overall market performance have little relevance to the future. Whether you are nearing retirement or just starting your investment career, the focus should be on where you are going, not on where you have been. It's the future you can create that matters, and the X-Factors can help you create the future you want.

PART I

Extraordinary Times

i. The state of our assets and debt

Why are these extraordinary times? Before we can devise exceptional strategies to take advantage of the investment conditions that exist today, we first need to understand the nature of the times we are living in now. A good place to start is by taking a look at the state of our assets and our debt.

Today, Canadians are saddled with more debt than at any time in our history. We are buried under high mortgages and massive credit card debt at record interest rates. In fact, it's almost amusing to think that while we are seeing record-low interest rates on money deposited in the bank—.05 percent on a daily interest savings account—credit card interest rates remain at 18.5 percent or more. Some department store cards actually carry interest rates as high as 28 percent, and that's non-deductible interest.

Canadians have also used the equity in their homes to "leverage up," borrowing against the perceived appreciation to buy more things. Today it seems that everyone just *has* to have that third car for the teenagers, that gas-guzzling SUV, that plasma screen TV, that state-of-the-art computer system. Meanwhile, we're paying more for things like gas to run those cars and electricity to power those electronic toys, plus more for car insurance and more in taxes. All of this "more" is the prime source of our rising debt load.

We know our debt load is high, and getting higher, but how do Canadians stand in terms of assets? Well, in terms of assets very little has changed in a very long time. Canadians are still not saving money at a very high rate relative to other nations. We do have lots of money locked away in RRSPs and RRIFs—about $400-billion—but that may expose us to massive taxation later on down the road. (We'll talk more about this in Section C: "A Life Less Taxing.")

If we look more closely at the state of our assets today, we find that, for most Canadians, our principal asset remains the same as it has always been: our principal residence. Every one percent rise in interest rates actually eliminates 10 percent of potential home buyers. But with the lowest interest rates in more than 40 years, people who would otherwise never have considered buying a home have been able to take the plunge, and there is a direct correlation between interest rates and the kind of home you can afford. The Central Mortgage and Housing Corporation has even eliminated the need to make a cash deposit on a house as long as the buyer can afford to pay the insurance premium, meaning many people today are buying real estate with "no money down." This is obviously quite an amazing situation, and one that is totally unique to our times.

How much do Canadians save from their after-tax income?

Year	Savings
1938	1.6%
1982	20.2%
1992	13%
2002	4.2%
2003	2%

Source: Statistics Canada

So where do most Canadians stand in terms of personal finances today? The truth is, most have not made much progress over the past two decades. Our largest asset is still our home, but we are still not building up enormous equity. Meanwhile, we still carry substantial liabilities and we have not made real, meaningful returns on our investments for the last decade. There are always exceptions, of course, but I think most Canadians would agree with that assessment to some degree. If you look at where you were a decade ago versus where you are today, after fees, taxes, and other liabilities are paid, is your net worth that much higher? If not, then you will probably also agree that most of the cures and clichés peddled by the investment industry over the past few years really haven't worked that well for most Canadian investors.

ii. Mass marketing of financial products and commodities

The mass marketing of financial products and commodities is something unique to our times. In our current marketplace, there are over 6,000 different mutual fund products to choose from, more products than there are stocks listed on the stock exchange, and Canadians have some $470-billion invested in them. In addition to those, we also have a massive proliferation of income trusts, with about $90-billion invested there. Along with that, there are 85 different equity markets competing for investors; thousands of different investment options; and now over 200 different hedge funds in Canada alone, compared to about a dozen five years ago.

With the ever increasing number of financial products and tax and investing strategies and concepts available today, it's no wonder most people are totally lost. The average investor doesn't know what to do with their money because there are just too many options to choose from.

With this proliferation of products and the mass media marketing that goes with it, we have essentially moved into the commodities stage of investment strategy. More and more we see business professionals moving from big companies like General Foods, Lever Brothers and Proctor & Gamble and going to work in marketing capacities in the mutual fund industry. In fact, Fidelity Mutual Funds of Boston has even said that mutual funds are essentially a commodity, with the value-added differentiation being the mutual fund company's name or brand, and not much else. In the mutual fund business, of course, exceptional performance is usually fleeting however, and, as the companies are always quick to point out, "past perform-ance is not an accurate predictor of future returns."

The fact is, if you take today's mass marketing of finan-cial products through mass media, then throw in the Internet, with its online and day trading, you have a recipe for investment-information overload. Today we have instant information sources like ROBTV and CNBC broadcasting information about what's going on in the business world and the financial markets "this minute," even "this second." Plus, we now have Internet access to those markets where we can get accurate, up-to-the-minute trade information from stock exchanges around the world, around the clock. In reality, though, the power of today's mass media to disseminate information actually ends up creating more chaos than clarity. There's just too much noise in the marketplace.

Do we really need all this financial information? The incessant obsession with the financial markets that has become so much a part of the world we now live in really borders on financial pornography—we tune in simply to satisfy our prurient interest in personal wealth. And our desire for new information is so strong, we don't tend to spend a lot of time processing each new piece of informa-tion before we move on to the next one. The focus is always on the new hot stock fund this very minute; what we should buy; what we should sell; what the financial gurus are going to tell us to do next.

Sadly, the vast majority of the financial information that floods into our heads every day is nothing more than pure nonsense. It is rare for any of this up-to-the-minute information to produce any real value over the long term and very few people can manage investments successfully in this kind of frantic trading environment anyway. For the average investor, more trading usually just means more tax and more fees paid to the various institutions that grow rich off of media-focused financial planning.

iii. Bulls and bears

The sad fact is, most people simply don't understand the true nature of bull and bear markets. Everyone understands that markets go up and markets go down, but they tend to have trouble understanding the nature of the market as it stands at a given time.

For example, look at the conditions that existed during the last bull market: we had the end of the Cold War; there were significant government surpluses; companies were expanding operations and investing large sums in new technology in order to increase productivity and remain "state of the art"; inflation fears were pretty well ended; interest rates were falling sharply; the Canadian dollar was rising dramatically; world oil prices were on the rise; and stock investing was the "in" thing to do. All the talk was about "hot fund," "best fund," flavour-of-the-month fund—everyone was buying stocks and everyone was going to get rich. Unfortunately, everyone conveniently forgot about the last time casual investors started to feel like that, back in the late 1920s.

During the recent bear market, of course, things looked quite different: we had an ongoing war on terrorism, which adds significantly to the cost of doing business; big U.S. government deficits were back, while here we had a great surplus; companies were putting off expansion plans and making investments in new technology; inflation fears were coming back due to high energy prices; interest rates were still low, but they were rising; although it appeared the Canadian dollar was getting stronger, the truth is the U.S. dollar dropped in value; foreign investors were selling off their North American stocks and stock investing was less important. In this kind of environment, investors tend to move toward the safety of capital and income strategies, which accounts for the recent mass proliferation of income trusts and principal protected notes.

Clearly, there are a lot of factors at play during both

bull and bear markets, and the challenge for the investor is learning how best to approach each situation—keeping in mind, of course, that no one has all the right answers all the time. Although we know markets go up and markets go down, that doesn't mean it is possible to accurately predict market futures. We can look at individual stocks and make an objective determination about what should be the superior investment in the long term, but predicting market outcomes with one-hundred-percent accuracy simply cannot be done.

iv. Analysts, accountants, and CEOs

Another factor to take into consideration when looking at the nature of markets is the performance of analysts, accountants, and CEOs. The last bear market was a very disturbing time in this regard because stocks tended to be driven by the opinions of analysts, earnings forecasts, and the assurances of managers and auditors. Needless to say, the opinions of these kinds of individuals have since fallen into disrepute and people no longer depend on that kind of information to make their investment decisions. In fact, highly publicized studies have shown that professional stock analysts have been no more successful in predicting markets or stock trends than someone with a dart board.

As if that were not bad enough, we now see accounting firms, formerly the cornerstone of integrity and probity in the financial marketplace, being exposed to substantial liability for making mistakes or, at worst, acting as co-conspirators in certain situations.

Then there is the problem of CEOs and senior executives being rewarded through stock options. This approach to executive remuneration turned the focus away from long-term profitability and the needs of the long-term shareholders—the people who actually owned and supported the business—and placed it on short-term profits more suited to speculative investors.

All of these factors have combined to create a divergence of interests in the current marketplace that has created significant long-term difficulty for investors. Thanks to the analysts, accountants, and CEOs, the real intent of buying stock in a company has been lost. When an investor buys a stock, what they are really buying is an interest in the future earnings potential and future value of the company. But if everyone's interests are not tied to that future potential, there's no chance that that company will succeed in the long term, and therefore no chance that the investment will be profitable in the long term.

v. Private pension funds and the Canada Pension Plan

Pension funds are increasingly finding themselves in great difficulty. In fact, there are some defined benefit pension funds that now have shortfalls of between 15 and 25 percent. A recent study by the Certified General Accountants (CGA) of Canada analyzed more than 800 defined-benefit plans across the country and found that these plans were running a combined deficit of some $160-billion.

How did this happen? The answer is as simple as it is disturbing: it happened because too many pension fund managers and analysts got caught up in the market hype. They moved away from conservative, capital protection strategies and into risky investment strategies in an effort to post big growth numbers for the fund and big bonuses for themselves.

Meanwhile, at the same time private pension funds were getting into difficulty, the government moved the Canada Pension Plan into equity markets and, once again, those great analysts and portfolio managers produced significant losses. On the bright side, however, due entirely to the massive rise in premiums to 9.9 percent of income, the Canada Pension Plan is now, for the first time, properly funded for the next 75 years. (Of course, if you happen to be in a government pension plan as a civil servant, you have an indexed pension for life which will certainly be properly funded by the taxpayer.)

Unfortunately, all Canadians will have to come to terms with the fact that one of our most cherished investment vehicles of safety, the pension fund, is no longer a sure bet. Today we are seeing large public companies looking to governments to bail out their insolvent pension funds and some companies are now cutting benefits in an attempt to keep their pension funds afloat. Pension fund contributors, meanwhile—the retired workers who contributed to company pension funds, in some cases, for decades—are now in very real danger of not receiving all the money they have coming to them. Government pension programs, on the other hand, may not have made some of the windfall profits of the private funds over the years, but at least they're properly funded for the long term.

vi. Changing demographics

Thanks to the current state of many private pension funds, we are starting to see another phenomenon new to the financial marketplace: individuals aged 55-plus who are at a loss as to what to do in order to fund their retirement. The demographics aren't helping the situation either. Today we have a large Baby Boom population that is now looking toward their impending retirement. As they move past age 55, their focus is moving away from asset appreciation and growth and into asset preservation. That means these investors are simply not going to be as active in the marketplace as they have been for the last 20 years or so. In fact, we will probably see historical returns gravitating back to five or six percent, and as a result the ability to grow wealth may be substantially curtailed.

The landscape is clearly shifting; the aging population, with its increasing demand for certain services, is going to create incredible change in the way we manage our money, and the time to embrace this change is now. Concepts like risk management, cost, taxation, and cash flow should be at the core of all financial planning today, placing the focus on where we are going, not on where we have been. Unfortunately, most investment strategies today are grounded in the past, focusing on how the markets reacted when the conditions were markedly different than they are today.

And just as the aging population is changing the way we manage our money, we are also changing the way we live as we age. First of all, thanks to modern medicine and healthier lifestyles, Canadians are living dramatically longer as individuals than ever before. That means we can hope to enjoy a longer, fuller life than previous generations, but it also means we are going to need more cash flow when we are older in order to live the kind of active lifestyle we want. In fact, what we need are multiple streams of cash flow—preferably tax-deferred, tax-reduced, or even tax-free—to fund our relative good health and active longevity. This requires a wholesale change in the way we plan for retirement.

So what exactly does retirement planning mean today? Does it mean simply putting away money for the future, like it did when our parents were still working? I don't believe it does. I think retirement planning today means ensuring that we don't outlive our money; it means we have the money to live the way we want for the duration of our lives. Obviously, if you have the money to live the way you want, and not just enough money to simply survive, your retirement promises to be much more enjoyable. You're going to be able to travel more, go back to school and take that art appreciation course you always wanted to take, redecorate your home, or help your children and grandchildren realize their dreams. Best of all, you'll be free of financial worry.

vii. Modern estate planning

If modern retirement planning means creating multiple streams of cash flow to ensure we don't run out of money before we run out of life, then estate planning has evolved from dealing with death and taxes to ensuring, once again, that the last phase of our life is as enjoyable as possible. The goal, therefore, should be to create a "living estate," one that meets your needs while you are still alive, rather than one that focuses on what you leave behind after you are dead.

This, of course, is not to say that you ignore the things that are the traditional focus of estate planning: you must still ensure that your wishes concerning your estate are carried out after you pass away, and that you look after your loved ones, including spouses, children, and grandchildren, and society in general in terms of charitable giving. The difference is those things should not be your only focus.

When we look at estate planning today, what we are really looking at is lifestyle. If you want to ensure you have enough money when you retire to have the lifestyle you want, the first thing you need to figure out is what that means in specific terms. First of all, where do you want to live? Do you want to continue to live in the large house where you raised your family? Do you want to downsize into an apartment or condominium? Do you want to maintain a cottage or vacation property? And what if you need to think about moving into some kind of assisted living retirement residence at some point? Have you planned for that?

Next, you need to ask yourself just how active you plan to be after you retire. Do you want to travel? Would you like to buy a new car or an RV and tour the country? Would you like to go back to school or take some re-education courses? What are your hobbies and how much do they cost? Golfing, sailing, skiing, gardening—they all cost money, and are you going to have enough to be as involved in your hobbies as you would like to be? Although some of these considerations might seem more trivial than others, the truth is they all involve important lifestyle decisions that will affect the quality of your life after you retire.

viii. Life, living, lifestyle—insurance

In order to incorporate all of these lifestyle dimensions in our estate planning, at some point we must turn our focus to insurance. In an uncertain world, insurance is simply the best way to protect the wealth you have for yourself and your family, both while you are living and after you have gone.

Believe it or not, the average Canadian household today spends between $3,500 to $6,000 a year on insurance, and those numbers are going to increase dramatically in the coming years for a number of reasons. Anyone with a house or a car knows that property/casualty rates have gone through the roof in recent years—a trend that promises to continue—and life insurance rates are climbing as well. In addition, the importance of insurance is also rising because insurance has become a critical tax-avoidance and cash-preservation vehicle for estate and retirement planning. There's no doubt insurance is a significant investment, but you have to ask yourself if it is an investment worth making.

When you stop and think about it, what we are really doing when we buy insurance is protecting a lifestyle. Term insurance is there to protect your family by ensuring their current lifestyle will be maintained should you, the principal breadwinner, die suddenly. At the same time, insurance is there to help us deal with many of life's tougher challenges—disability, long-term care, critical illness, catastrophic loss. Dealing with disability issues is critical to estate planning because, statistically, we are five times more likely to become disabled between the ages of 20 and 55 than we are to die during that period. In addition, insurance also offers estate-preservation options.

Simply put, insurance and estate planning go hand-in-hand today. Life, living, lifestyle, insurance—they've all become one: another new dimension of our changing times.

ix. Terrorism and security

Clearly, the security challenges we are confronted with today are different from those we were confronted with a decade ago. The world has become a far more complex place, and that means ensuring our security, both personal and business, has become a far more difficult and much more expensive proposition.

Insurance rates have gone up, and travel has become much more complicated and expensive for everybody because we are all now paying "risk" premiums to cover increased security costs. Businesses, meanwhile, must cut deeper than ever into their profits to ensure their assets are adequately protected from theft or destruction, and developers can't build any kind of building today unless the insurance for that building is in place before a shovel goes in the ground.

There's no denying the fact that the threat of world terrorism and the fear for personal security it creates are having a direct impact on our lifestyle choices. Security has become a very real factor in determining what we can do, where we can go, who can travel where, and all of this is new and disturbing for most people. Ironically, all of this liability creates opportunity for people who specialize in mitigating risk, and companies in the security and insurance businesses are reporting record profits.

This state of constant vigilance is certainly not the best environment in which to live and do business, but it's something we are all going to have to get used to dealing with for the foreseeable future. The ever-evolving security environment in our changing world just emphasizes, once again, that we are living in very extraordinary times.

x. Mergers, acquisitions, and consolidations

Mergers and acquisitions have always been a way of life in the business world, but consolidations in the financial services industry over the past few years have led to progressively fewer choices for consumers.

In the insurance industry, for example, we have moved from as many as 130 insurance companies in this country a decade ago down to perhaps two dozen major carriers today. Meanwhile, in the financial planning industry we have seen massive consolidation of financial planning firms. Fewer and fewer firms means fewer and fewer choices, in terms of both suppliers and products, and more salespeople tied to selling in-house products to maximize profits for the big company at your expense.

It also stands to economic reason that fewer choices inevitably leads to higher prices, and, in many cases, less value and poorer service. When companies don't have to fight as hard to attract and maintain customers, they have no incentive to be "customer service driven." In this kind of environment, companies tend to think of marketing as simply launching new products that sell rather than meeting the customer's needs, desires, demands, and changing lifestyle by developing and offering products that are designed to do just that.

When the company's focus is simply on selling the product rather than on improving the life of the customer, the product becomes a simple commodity, just as mutual funds and most other investment products have become simple commodities in today's financial services marketplace. Some sales representatives seem more interested in getting rich at your expense than they are in serving your needs as a customer and ensuring that you are better off for having done business with them.

Actually, when I look at the state of the financial services industry today, I'm reminded of a line from Woody Allen's film *A Midsummer Night's Sex Comedy.* When someone asks Allen's character what he does for a living, he replies: "I work on Wall Street; I manage other people's money—until it's all gone."

Unfortunately, that line would be funnier if it weren't so true. In many cases today, "financial planning services" is simply a euphemism for turning *your* wealth into *their* wealth. I often tell people to ask themselves one key question: Who made more money last year off of your investments, you or your bank? You or your financial advisory firm? These are critical questions to consider, especially in a financial services marketplace where mergers, acquisitions, and consolidations are resulting in less choice, poorer service, higher costs and, most important, lower returns for you.

xi. Advisors, mediation, and self-directed investing

The financial advisory network exploded at an incredible rate between 1988 and 1995, right about the same time we saw a massive proliferation of investment products. Factors such as the change in RRSP rules, allowing for contributions of $12,000 and $13,500 and moving up to 18 percent of earned income, and the development of the deferred sales charge combined to create a wholesale shift of the focus of the financial services industry toward investment retirement planning and the explosion of the RRSP concept.

There is no denying the fact that the RRSP strategy worked very well for the financial services industry, and a lot of advisory firms made a lot of money off of it. The movement was based on intermediation, where the investor would work with a financial advisor to create a detailed financial plan. To be quite honest though, most of the financial advisors working in the financial services industry during that approximately 15-year period that marked the heyday of the RRSP were really just mutual fund salespeople. Very few did proper financial planning, or "holistic" financial planning as it is sometimes called. Holistic financial planning meant that the advisor analyzed every aspect of the customer's personal financial life: cash, cost, risk, tax, and cash flow. Once they had a clear picture of the customer's financial position, the advisor would then sit down and draw up detailed investment, risk, tax, and estate plans that were integrated together into a kind of "total concept" financial plan.

As the marketplace evolved, however, that kind of holistic financial planning became a rarity and the focus of the industry switched to investment strategy, with a special emphasis being placed on chasing the hot funds and the hot stocks. Instead of "plan, plan, plan," the mantra of the financial advisor became "trade, trade, trade." The result of this switch in focus, unfortunately, was that many investors

> A visitor to New York asked her guide who owned all the yachts moored off Battery Park.
>
> "Why, the Wall Street bankers and brokers, of course," replied the New Yorker.
>
> "In that case," said the visitor, "where are all their customers' yachts?"

became hopelessly entrapped in their advisor's in-house investment products.

Toward the late 1990s, the process of intermediation changed again. With the evolution of online trading and Internet day trading, we entered a period of, if you will, "disintermediation," with investors trying to do everything themselves. RRSPs became self-directed instead of advisor-directed. The go-it-alone approach worked for the odd investor, but more often than not the results were disastrous. Most investors simply couldn't unravel the complexities of the various investment products on their own.

It also doesn't help that the whole investment market-place is designed specifically to encourage trading. Inexperienced investors are bombarded constantly with up-to-the-minute updates from the TSE, the NYSE and NASDAQ; mutual fund advertisements and marketing campaigns; and "hot stock" tips and advisor reports coming in via e-mail. This constant investment hype screams out, "buy, buy, buy," and "sell, sell, sell," pushing investors to "act now" or miss out. Sure, some investors profit in this kind of overcharged marketplace, but mostly what gets generated is more and more transaction fees for investment firms, more taxes on investors' money, and, too often, investor losses.

Today, happily, more and more people are learning to overlook the media hype and take a more balanced approach to investment planning, so the self-directed investor is actually making a comeback. But while more investors are moving toward self-direction in order to reduce costs, there is still a role for the holistic financial planner who knows what proper financial planning means. Unfortunately, there are currently not many financial planners like that out there, but the ones that remain are doing an excellent job for investors wise enough to search them out and work with them. These planners do a better job for their clients because they understand that financial planning is not just about investing; it's about managing risk, cost, cash flow, and taxation, and integrating all these elements into a single financial plan.

xii. Costs up/taxes up/risk up/transactions up

If your overall costs are up, that probably means your revenue and return are down, because it's the net after-tax and after-cost return that counts. In fact, Professor Moshe Milevsky of York University's Schulich School of Business has pointed out that it is after-tax, after-cost, and after-inflation return that matters. That's the real return we like to tell people about. That's the money you get to spend on things you wouldn't otherwise be able to afford. Today, however, that little extra in your pocket is under attack—costs are increasing everywhere; taxes continue to rise; and net disposable income is, in fact, on the decline, especially in comparison to that of Americans.

Given the current environment, it has now become prudent to ask yourself why you are doing the things you are doing in terms of your financial planning. If the current focus of financial planning is on transactions, and the cost of performing transactions is rising, then the level of risk associated with that approach is rising as well. Then add to that the increasing level of risk in general in the world associated with war, terrorism, security concerns, and economic uncertainty. When all of these things are taken into account, the current environment is challenging, to say the least, for the average investor—risk is up; the number and cost of transactions is up; taxes are up; everyday living costs are up. As all of these various factors go up, your return, your wealth, your security go down. In a financial planning environment such as the one we find ourselves in today, it is very easy for average investors to lose control of their financial destiny.

Faced with this reality, any investment strategy, any holistic approach to managing finances, must address what I believe to be the four core elements of good financial planning: cost, cash, risk, and cash flow. We must work to curtail, rather than incur, transactions. We must strive to remain in control of the costs we incur in every area of our lives. And, finally, we must do everything we can to control the taxes we pay.

PART 2
Where Are the Knowledge Providers?

i. The research gap

The thing that empowers the average investor the most is the ability to make informed decisions. Staying informed involves two essential elements: first, investors should work synergistically with an investment advisor; second, they must make good use of the information channels available to them. Making optimum use of these two resources will allow investors to make better decisions about the financial factors that they can control.

Why is knowledge so pivotal to financial success? Well, as we've said before, nobody can control the stock market (although every once in a while some dubious individuals like to think they can). Most sensible investors know that it is impossible to consistently make accurate predictions about overall stock market trends or to predict the long-term performance for individual stocks.

But this fact presents investors with a conundrum: if it is impossible to control financial markets, what *can* investors control? Well, the truth is, the only thing investors can control is their level of knowledge about the marketplace. There is no substitute for current, accurate knowledge when it comes to making informed decisions about assessing risk, determining costs, minimizing taxation, and improving cash flow. It may sound clichéd, but in terms of financial planning, knowledge really does equal power.

And speaking of clichés, it is an unfortunate truth about the current financial planning industry that too many investors today are making decisions based not on their knowledge of the marketplace, but on marketing slogans. To be fair, however, the relevant data are not always readily available; there is actually very little empirical research done in Canada today on financial markets and market activity. Our situation stands in stark contrast to the United States, where many leading colleges and universities have established endowed research chairs dedicated to the study of financial markets, many funded by the mutual fund and insurance industries.

There are a handful of academics who publish studies on the financial planning industry in this country, but they are the exception, mostly because funding to conduct this kind of research is simply not available. One of those exceptions is the Fraser Institute in Vancouver, which does research on topics such as the impact of investment costs and taxation on investors. But the Fraser Institute is generally perceived as a "right-wing think tank," rather than an unbiased, independent research organization. This is unfortunate, because I have found the research conducted by the Fraser Institute to be highly reliable.

Another good source of useful research on the financial markets in Canada is the Toronto-based C.D. Howe Institute, led by Dr. Jack Mintz, professor of taxation at the Rotman School of Management at the University of Toronto. The C.D. Howe Institute routinely produces very reliable and totally objective empirical studies, mostly on issues related to taxation. In recent years, the C.D. Howe Institute has published studies on our tax system, the decline of disposable income, the failure of pension plans, the impact of RRSPs on taxation, and the spectre of poverty that hangs over many Canadian seniors.

Some of the best current research refuting the "mutual fund" approach to financial planning has been conducted by Dr. Moshe Milevsky and his colleagues at York University's Schulich School of Business. Based on their research, Professor Milevsky and his team have developed a very basic approach to financial planning that stands in clear opposition to most conventional financial planning wisdom. Putting all of the noise in the marketplace aside, they argue that there is really only one thing that counts for the investor at the end of the day, and that is RAT— Real After-Tax return. What was your real after-tax return last month, or last year, after inflation and costs, on all your investments? It's a refreshing view, but not one you are likely to hear or read about in the mainstream media.

Unfortunately, the excellent research on the Canadian financial planning marketplace conducted at places like the Fraser Institute, the C.D. Howe Institute, and York University receives far less attention in the media than it truly deserves. The reason for this is that much of this research is less than supportive of the "mutual fund" approach to financial planning, and the Canadian media are not eager to do anything to disrupt the abundant advertising support it currently receives from the entrenched mutual fund industry.

> If you had invested $1,000 in stock 50 years ago, you would have amassed **$212,000** based on the market's average return of over 11% per year.
>
> However, if you factor in the impact of inflation over that time, the amount would be just **$31,000**.
>
> Subtract a further 2% per year for investment costs and it's **$11,600**.
>
> Finally, subtract another 2% per year for taxes, and you are left with just **$4,300**.

Because of the dearth of financial planning research in Canada, and thus our dangerous reliance on long-term U.S. studies, most investors really don't understand the nature of investment strategy in the Canadian context. The problem with relying on U.S. research is that it does not present an accurate picture of the Canadian financial planning reality: we have different regulations governing our business and investment activities; our markets operate differently; we have a different economic structure; we have different taxation rules; we have a different demographic makeup; and we have different needs and attributes in terms of things like health, longevity, and lifestyle requirements. As a result, empirical research done on the U.S. financial planning marketplace, while certainly well done and of some general interest to Canadian investors, is simply not detailed and specific enough to meet our needs. It would certainly not be prudent for a Canadian investor to make any kind of financial planning decision based on U.S. research, regardless of the source.

This "research gap" is precisely why so much of the market "knowledge" currently peddled in the Canadian financial planning industry is suspect. It is common to see financial planning product providers citing this study and that study about certain industries and funds and stocks, but few investors take the time to nail down the source of this research. Often the studies cited by product providers come from the U.S., and many are generated by U.S. product providers themselves. Rarely, if ever, do you see a financial planning company or an investment product provider citing or—God forbid—funding independent research on financial markets in Canada.

But, to be fair, financial planning companies and investment product providers are not really in business to be "knowledge providers." In fact, when one thinks about it, these companies have nothing to gain by disseminating current, accurate knowledge of the investment marketplace at no cost to consumers. These companies are quite content to put out "insider reports" and newsletters that are really just promotional materials in disguise, providing no real investment insight.

Meanwhile, training programs for Canadian financial advisors often involve bringing up a U.S. investment expert to talk about how they work with customers in Texas or California, which, of course, is of no real use to a financial advisor working in this country. The goal for the company, though, is not to teach their advisors how to do the best job they can for their Canadian clients given the realities of their investment marketplace; it is to give their advisors the marketing skills they will need to attract high-net-worth investors and to get their clients to buy their in-house investment products. They want to train their advisors to sell products, not provide knowledge.

ii. A fanatical fixation on clichés

How does the financial planning industry get away with not providing knowledge to their customers? They do it by overwhelming them with a constant barrage of marketing clichés. We've all heard them: hot fund; top fund; a rising tide raises all boats; asset allocation; diversify or die, etc., etc. And although investment advisors love to chant these mantras ad nauseam to their clients, most are simply not true (and we will go in to more detail about that later on). It's the oldest trick in the propagandist's handbook: empty marketing slogans just take on the appearance of truth through repetition.

Unfortunately, when people hear or read these clichés in the media, they repeat them to other uninformed people because they believe it makes them sound like they know what they're talking about, and that generates more misinformation. But an endless succession of clichés coming from anybody's mouth, especially a financial planner's, usually means one or more of the following: a) they have no knowledge; b) they have not been properly trained; c) they have not studied the good available research; d) they are acting in the best interests of the product providers, trying to separate your money from you and transfer it over to them in the form of transaction fees.

It is accurate to say that the financial planning industry today is built on nothing more than a flimsy foundation of marketing slogans. For that reason, it is also accurate to say that the vast majority of financial planning decisions made today are based more on ignorance and generalization than on detailed, specific, empirical knowledge. And because financial planning firms have moved away from the provision of knowledge, there is now a lack of understanding among financial planning advisors themselves about what investors need to know.

The most important duty of the financial advisor is to educate clients so that they can be empowered to make informed decisions about their financial future. But most financial advisors today are not equipped to perform that duty. Their goal should be to secure the client's long-term business by rewarding them financially through the provision of knowledge, rather than to lock the client in through the sale of in-house investment products. Somewhere along the line, though, the financial planning industry lost sight of that goal.

Over the years, I have gathered the best empirical research available at the time to develop various financial planning resources: *What the Rich Do*—where I looked at the investment strategies employed by Canada's top one percent of wage earners; *Your Family's Money*—a study of 10,000 Canadian families, the good, the bad, and the ugly; and *Death and Taxes*—a detailed "think tank" analysis that brought together four estate planning lawyers and four tax accountants to study the protection of capital assets in the estate. With every one of these series, my objective was to provide detailed knowledge so that the general investor could learn and benefit from the success of others in a uniquely Canadian context. Sadly, very little of the information contained in these resources is accessed by the average investor, so they continue to live by the clichés and hope for the best.

PART 3

The Past Versus The Future

i. Are Canadians financially healthy?

Just how are Canadians doing in terms of their financial well being? The short answer is: not so good, especially when it comes to debt. In fact, what we should really be asking ourselves is how we managed to get into so much debt in the first place. There are several answers to this question—conspicuous consumption, ignorance, greed—but the one thing that ties all of these together is the fact we have allowed ourselves to get sucked in by the media and its endless marketing pitches, hype, and promotions.

It is really not that surprising that so many people end up with unmanageable debt loads, not when you consider the fact that we live in a world today where anyone coming out of high school can get their own credit card. Impressionable teenagers are ripe pickings for the credit card companies because they tend to look only as far as the next item they want to possess, forgetting completely about the astronomical interest rate they have to pay to finance that credit card purchase. Add that credit card debt to other expenses commonly incurred by young people, like rent, a student loan, a car lease or loan, and you soon have a recipe for financial disaster. In fact, it's quite common for young graduates today to come out of college or university with a debt load of $20,000, $30,000, or even $40,000. And that's long before they even consider purchasing their first home.

There's no doubt about it: indebtedness has become the focus of too many financial plans today, and that is simply because going into debt allows us to live well beyond our means. What people are really doing, though, is burying themselves in liability and pouring thousands upon thousands of dollars every year down the drain in the form of interest payments—non-deductible in this country—and fees to various financial institutions.

So how did we get here? Simply put, we bought into the hype. People today aren't interested in just living their life; they want to live a certain "lifestyle," and they want it all right now. Few people today are willing to take the old, time-honoured route where they work and save for their future purchases by controlling their expenditures and being frugal and disciplined with their hard-earned money. That old "Protestant work ethic" approach to life seems horribly antiquated in this day and age. No, the whole idea of personal restraint has gone by the wayside in most areas of life, and financial planning is no exception.

ii. What do we actually have?

It is always a useful exercise when trying to figure out how our finances get in the condition they are in to look at how we actually live our lives. In their lifetime, the average Canadian today will spend about 141,000 hours sleeping; 85,000 hours working; 81,000 hours watching television; about 10,000 hours commuting back and forth to work; and, regrettably, only about 1,600 hours having sex. Now, compare those numbers with the fact that the average Canadian will spend only 160 hours in their entire lifetime on investment, tax, and estate planning.

The truth is we spend just a fraction of our time thinking about the decisions that will have the greatest effect on the quality of our life, especially of the last 30 years of our life. This is, or at least should be, a shocking number for people to consider. The good news is it is never too late to take greater control over the amount of time you spend on investment, tax, and estate planning.

The next important thing to take a serious look at is where we actually stand in terms of our finances—that is what we have, what we own, and where it came from. For example, over the course of the last 11 years or so, the personal disposable income of Canadians has declined from 79.3 percent of the U.S. level of disposable income down to 74.5 percent, largely due to taxation. Personal income also declined dramatically over that period because investment returns declined. In 2003, investment income actually declined about 12.5 percent, despite a turnaround in equity markets. Record-low interest rates, of course, have also had an adverse effect on many investors.

Discouraging? Well, consider the fact that it has actually been impossible for an un-tax-sheltered GIC or savings bond to produce a return over the last 30 years. That's right—after increasing taxes and inflation have been taken into consideration, it was *mathematically impossible* to make any return on your money; yet we now have record amounts in this country invested in such vehicles. So we are clearly working from a state of ignorance.

If we look at more recent studies, like the survey conducted in 2003 by the *National Post*, we find that the average household income in Canada is around $60,000. That study also found that the average family spends about $11,000 a year on shelter; some $6,500 on food; $3,500 on insurance; and about $2,500 on clothing. They will also spend about 20 percent or more of their income on taxes, or about $13,276 per year on average. Personal savings, unfortunately, are not of any great significance, and we give next to nothing to charity—the average Canadian family donated less than $696 to registered charities in 2002.

When it comes to retirement savings plans, the average Canadian family currently has about $120,000 saved for retirement. In addition, we have maybe $30,000 or $40,000 in other investments and our largest single asset, valued at an average of about $150,000, is our principal residence. Various types of debt—credit card, mortgage, lines of credit, car loans, student loans—represent well over $120,000 in liabilities for the average family. This places the net worth of the average Canadian family at about $250,000.

Now if this sounds like a significant amount, it is important to remember that the bulk of that worth is in the principal residence. This is fine, in as much as the principal residence is a "tax-free" investment that remains tax-free forever. However, the average Canadian family still does not do much in terms of tax planning, and taxes, meanwhile, continue to rise. A report issued by the Fraser Institute in February of 2004 showed that a Canadian family earning the average annual income of $60,000 spent about 47 percent of their total disposable income on various taxes—federal, provincial, municipal. It's a shocking number, but that's where your money goes.

Faced with that grim reality, how do we begin to reduce the tax bite that is taking so much out of our disposable income? First of all, taxpayers can't do much about their municipal taxes, simply because municipal taxes are usually based on the assessed value of their principal residence. Short of appealing the assessment or moving, your municipal taxes are basically fixed. We can, however, do something about the amount of provincial taxes we pay because provincial taxes are usually a percentage of the federal tax. So, if you paid $17,500 in income tax last year and you could reduce your taxes by 20 percent, that would be $3,500 extra in your pocket; imagine what you could do with that money. Controlling the amount of tax we pay is something we know we can do to improve our financial position. And why shouldn't we, especially when the federal surplus is running at about $9-billion annually?

> Average gross family income in Canada (adjusted for inflation) :
> 1993: **$67,000**   2003: **$73,000**
>
> Taxes (as % of gross family income):
> 1993: **43.6%**   2003: **48.3%**
>
> Increase in average after-tax income in Canada between 1991 and 2003: **$157**
>
> Source: Fraser Institute

But what else can we do that we are not currently doing to improve our financial position? According to a recent report by the C.D. Howe Institute, if you have less than $100,000 in your RRSP when you retire, it creates nothing but claw-backs and progressive liabilities, ultimately making that approach more punitive than progressive. Therefore, if we continue to rely on the great investment strategies created by the mutual fund industry—asset allocation, market timing, stock picking, sector rotating, momentum playing, etc., etc.—we are probably going to be more successful in separating ourselves from our returns than we will be in saving money for retirement.

Also, Canadians have just not been very disciplined in terms of saving their money. We don't seem to see the logic in putting away enough in order to maintain our lifestyle after retirement. The 2005 average savings rate among Canadians of about zero percent of earned income simply won't cut it for the long term. We won't be able to meet even modest investment targets at that rate, because after you consider changing factors like the increasing cost of taxation, the rising cost of energy, and the rising cost of property and casualty insurance, few families out there have any money left over to invest.

In the 2004 Budget, the government attempted to provide an incentive to save for families earning less than $70,000 through Canadian Educational Savings Grants, but the effort was really a waste of time. The impact of this move will be minimal because few, if any, of these families will have any money left over, after they pay their taxes and other expenses, to invest in a Registered Educational Savings Plan (RESP) in order to qualify for the federal grants. They just don't have it.

It is also important to consider the fact that most long-term projections, hypothetical as they are, suggest that real returns in the equity markets will be weak over the next 10 to 15 years, averaging, maybe, around five percent. If this proves to be the case, many investors may end up being very disappointed with the performance of their investments over that period.

In addition, other studies show that average income has risen, at best, insignificantly, and at worst, not at all. And because we are consuming so much more of our earned income today just in the cost of living, it is going to become increasingly difficult to increase the small proportion of our income we currently manage to save and invest for retirement.

Granted, these facts are not encouraging. But they are facts nonetheless, and we must face our current financial realities if we ever hope to formulate a workable financial plan for the future. It is also an unavoidable reality that all of these increasing financial pressures have resulted in a decrease in the standard of living for most Canadians. While that may not be too disturbing, or even noticeable, in the short term, it will certainly become increasingly so in the long term. In fact, when compared to our American neighbours, our average income and standard of living in Canada is in quite a rapid decline, and has been for some time.

And, as the aging population continues to push up the cost of our government-run health care system, Canadians can no longer look to Ottawa to bail them out in retirement. The money is already accounted for, so it's not going to be there for individuals who did not have the foresight to save for their own retirement. Given these realities, you can expect your standard of living to continue to decline as you get older—that is unless you are prepared to take control of your own financial future right now and do some real, holistic financial planning.

PART 4

What the Rich Do

i. Are the rich really different?

Back in 1996 and '97, we conducted a series of empirical studies through our non-profit research institute, the Canadian Institute for Personal Finance. These studies were underwritten by Dun & Bradstreet Canada and AGF Mutual Funds, but we were given complete control over which areas of personal finance we would look at and how the research would be conducted.

Using investor databases provided by Dun & Bradstreet and AGF, we did telephone interviews with literally thousands of "wealthy" Canadians right across the country. For the purposes of the study, wealthy individuals were defined as those with incomes in excess of $150,000 per year and a net worth of at least $500,000, excluding their principal residence. The goal of the study was to determine whether or not these individuals take similar approaches to investment, retirement, estate, and tax planning, and whether or not these approaches differ from those taken by individuals who are not as well off.

Predictably, the researchers found that most of the individuals interviewed for the study tended to be entrepreneurs, professionals, executives, or owner/managers. They also found that only a small proportion of the interviewees were inheritors of wealth; for the most part, they had earned their money themselves.

After analyzing the data generated by the interviews, we found that, generally speaking, the subjects of the study tended to be very conservative, even passive, investors. It quickly became apparent that the top priority for these high-net-worth individuals was not so much the accumulation of more wealth as it was the preservation of existing wealth at all costs.

What does that tell us? It tells us, first and foremost, that rich people want to stay rich. In fact, most wealthy individuals are not interested at all in making high risk/high return investments. If they can get six, seven, or eight percent return on their investments, most high-net-worth individuals are absolutely ecstatic. They don't look for the big home run. Their focus is not just on maximizing return; it is on maximizing capital preservation by minimizing risk. They do this by incorporating proper risk management strategies into their investment planning and constantly working to minimize the taxes they pay (keeping in mind, of course, that all of their tax planning is by the book—nothing exaggerated, nothing omitted). The goal is safety and security for the long term.

ii. How do they do it?

Clearly, rich people do things differently, and that reality has been exposed again and again in our ongoing research. To begin with, certain basic concepts appear to be inherent in people who are financially successful: a regular pattern of saving; personal spending discipline; realistic lifestyle expectations; and—believe it or not—the use of common sense. Unlike many middle-class investors, high-net-worth individuals also seem to have a very clear understanding of the investment maxim, "If it seems too good to be true, it probably is."

Contrary to popular belief, the investment game plan for most wealthy individuals is actually very simple: do a few things right and avoid mistakes. Their investment portfolios tend to be very focused and concentrated, containing perhaps only eight to ten stocks. Obviously this approach contradicts many of the investment models currently in vogue, including asset allocation, stock picking, market timing, and sector rotating. In fact, high-net-worth individuals seem to make a conscious effort to avoid falling into the trap of the "next new thing" in investment strategy.

Along with their conservative, concentrated approach to investing, the other factor that sets the rich apart is their ability to save money at an amazing rate relative to the average person. If the average Canadian is currently saving at a rate of slightly above zero percent of earned income per year, high-net-worth Canadians are saving at a rate of 22 percent of earned income per year. Obviously, this is an extraordinarily high savings rate, and the wealthy can manage it because they simply don't do the things middle- and low-income Canadians do: they avoid impulse buying and they avoid high levels of indebtedness, especially credit card and other high-interest debt.

We also know that, along with their normal income, high-net-worth individuals also often generate additional cash flow from other sources, like real estate. Their investment portfolio is usually focused on bonds, insurance products, and a small number of blue-chip stocks that they hold for the long term—dividends are very important. The rich also invest heavily in their children and their children's education, thus ensuring that the next generation will have greater earning potential than the general population.

Therefore, while it is true that the rich have greater means than the vast majority of the population, it is also true that the rich make a greater effort to live within their means. They also rely heavily on legal, tax, and financial advisors to help ensure that they continue to keep the wealth they have.

How focused are the rich on keeping their money? Research has shown that some 60 percent of high-net-worth individuals have avoided active stock trading in the last few years. The majority of these individuals tend to follow a 10- to 20-year buy-and-hold investment strategy. And because they have realistic expectations of a six to eight percent annualized growth rate for their investments, they avoid gambling on high-flying stocks. High-net-worth individuals are more apt to stick with a proven winner in their portfolio than they are to rush to the next "growth asset."

The fact that the rich do things differently is never more apparent than when you look at statistics related to active wealth creation. Over the course of the last decade, 90 percent of the growth in personal wealth in North America has gone to the top five percent of asset holders. How did they do it? Well, most of the investors in that top five percent made their investments before 1992, at the very beginning of the bull market and long before the vast majority of casual investors started pouring money into the equity markets via mutual funds. The bull market peaked in March of 2000, which was also the number one month in history for mutual fund investing in Canada. That means that the majority of investors put their money in at the top of the market; buying high only to sell low down the road. And who do you think was selling off their stocks at the top of the market after investing at the bottom years ago? No wonder the rich keep getting richer.

Many wealthy investors obviously had the right financial plan in place back in 1992, and they continue to do the right things today. First and foremost, by cultivating reasonable expectations of returns, they avoid gambling on high-risk stocks. They know that building a realistic model of returns over time is at the core of holistic financial planning. And because they have the discipline to stick to the longer-term time horizons in their financial plan, they avoid exposing themselves to the "get rich quick" investments that many casual investors fall victim to.

It is often very tempting for a casual investor, who is perhaps only five or six years away from retirement, to put money into a short-term, high-risk investment in an attempt to "top up" their retirement savings with a quick 30 or 40 percent return at the last minute. Unfortunately, these types of investments fail at least as often as they work out. More important, though, five or six years from retirement is not the time to be gambling with your money.

High-net-worth individuals know this, and they act accordingly. They don't pay constant attention to the ups and downs of the market and they block out the marketing noise from the investment industry. Instead, they concentrate on the value of their assets and adhere to an investment strategy that is going to, at a minimum, maintain that value for the long term. This long-term approach, in turn, rules out irrational, short-term financial planning and eliminates irrational decision-making. Protecting capital and maintaining existing wealth at all costs is what matters most.

There is an old Bahamian proverb that goes: "Ignore the noise of the fish market; just look at the cost and quality of the fish provided." Obviously, the logic of that saying isn't lost on high-net-worth individuals; in fact, it is one of their core financial planning concepts. That's why the rich are more successful investors and will continue to be so. The good news is you don't have to be rich to benefit from that logic. Anyone who takes the same approach to their own financial planning will inevitably do better. We can actually learn more from watching successful people than we can from talking to our banker, the shopping mall financial advisor, or the talking-head investment "experts" in the media.

If your goal is to be financially successful, and I think we all share that goal, then your first task is to find out what financially successful people have to say about financial planning, and the resources are out there to allow you to do just that. A book like *Common Stocks and Uncommon Profits*, by the late Phil Fisher, is a good place to start, as is *The Intelligent Investor* by Benjamin Graham. Also, familiarize yourself with the basic concepts behind Warren Buffett's investment success with Berkshire Hathaway Inc.

If you look at what these individuals have done, how

they do their analysis, and what they recommend, you will see that they don't have some magic formula for financial success. In fact, there is nothing really special about their approach to investing: it is simple, disciplined, long-term, and forward-thinking. Yet they became fabulously successful while the vast majority of casual investors continued to spiral downward. Obviously there's a powerful lesson to be learned here, and you should always learn from success, not from failure.

Think you're a rational investor? Try this test:

Problem 1: You have $1,000 to invest. Choose between
(a) a 50 percent chance to gain another $1,000 and a 50 percent chance to gain nothing, or
(b) a sure gain of $500.

Problem 2: You have $2,000 to invest. Choose between
(a) a 50 percent chance to lose $1,000 and a 50 percent chance to lose nothing, or
(b) a sure loss of $500.

In a study by economists Daniel Kahneman of Princeton University and Richard Thaler of the University of Chicago, in Problem 1, 84 percent of test subjects chose (b). In Problem 2, 69 percent chose (a).

The odd thing about these results is that if the majority of subjects opt for the sure $1,500 of choice (b) in Problem 1, the majority therefore ought to opt for the same sure $1,500 payout from choice (b) in Problem 2. Instead, the majority of subjects were willing to take the risk to try to "break even" when the problem was framed in terms of losses.

According to Kahneman and Thaler, this study suggests that, irrationally, people feel differently about losing than they do about gaining, even if either choice produces the same outcome.

PART 5

The Power of Simplicity: Less Can Produce More

i. What can you control?

I believe that if you can control the controllables, you will perform dramatically better financially in the long term.

As I have said, no one can accurately predict long-term stock market trends and no one can predict the long-term performance of individual equities, at least not with any degree of consistency. In fact, very few strategic investors, whether they were using market timing strategies, sector rotating strategies (where they try to guess the next hot sector), or some other approach, have enjoyed any kind of consistent success. Most sector rotators have actually missed five of the last seven sector changes. With success rates like that, it is fair to say that these glorified investment strategies are really no better than guessing when it comes to predicting investment outcomes.

However, investing is not about guessing; *gambling* is about guessing. Even the most unsophisticated investor knows that their money should be riding on something more than a hunch. The primary goal of every good investment strategy should be to eliminate the guesswork, because the fewer guesses you make, the less risk there is inherent in your financial plan. And eliminating risk is the best way to simplify your financial life and improve your investment performance.

High-net-worth investors put a lot of stock in the concept that less often produces more. Research shows that a focused, concentrated approach to investing will, in fact, result in better returns in the long term. It does this by generating less risk, less cost, and less tax, thus resulting in better cash flow. Why? Because those are the only controllable elements in holistic financial planning.

So less really can mean more—that's the X-Factor. Less of the negative factors produces more of the positive one: more cash for you. Less means more because you control the amount of risk you take on, and risk is just another name for the potential to lose money. Less means more because you control the amount of taxes and financial service fees you pay.

Because the rich are not active traders and are always looking to control cost every step of the way, they usually end up incurring costs only for things that make financial sense in the long term. For example, say you had money invested in an income trust mutual fund that was producing a 9.5 percent cash flow and someone came to you and said they would make that income tax-free at a cost of 50 basis points to you. Would it be worth it to incur the cost of the 50 basis points on your assets to avoid 46 percent tax? The answer, of course, is yes; obviously, that would make financial sense. And that is what happens when you buy the fund inside a universal life insurance policy.

But what if, on the other hand, someone came to a 30-year-old and said, "Give me one percent of your income every year for the rest of your working life, and I will guarantee you against loss"? In that case, no matter what happens, the 30-year-old is guaranteed to at least get their money back, and that is essentially what a segregated mutual fund offers. But is that a smart, long-term investment for a 30-year-old? Probably not.

For a 75-year-old investor, however, with a much higher probability of mortality in the near term, that kind of investment might make perfect sense. If an older person can invest money at no risk to themselves, is it worth paying one percent a year to have an absolute guarantee that they, at the very least, won't lose any money? Generally speaking, the answer in that case is probably yes.

As we can see from the preceding examples, any given investment is not necessarily right for every investor. Each individual investor must view each investment opportunity through the spectrum of their particular circumstances and only make investments that make absolute sense "for them." Still, no matter the age or the personal financial circumstances of the investor, the core considerations of holistic financial planning remain the same: protecting capital, reducing risk, improving cash flow, and cutting taxes. Those are the controllable factors, and taking control is the essence of proper financial planning.

ii. Creating an X-Factor investment model strategy

If we wanted to produce an X-Factor financial model, what would it look like? In the simplest terms, we would have to focus on investments that will do the most for us with the least amount of risk, the least tax, and the best cash flow at the lowest possible cost.

For example, it is probably not worth buying an investment product that carries a fee of more than two percent, not unless it guaranteed a return of twelve to fifteen percent, thus ensuring a secure cash flow for the investor over the term of the investment. Some asset-backed investment products, like those tied to assets such as existing car leases, offer a fairly solid guarantee of cash flow for investors in spite of high management fees. However, any mutual fund product that carries a management expense ratio, or MER, of over two percent is simply not worth it.

Surprisingly enough, empirical research generated in 2004 shows that among actively traded mutual funds, some with the highest management fees historically have produced the better returns. Logic dictates that higher fees should result in lower returns because the fund would have to do extraordinarily well to make up for its huge costs, yet some funds have done just that. But those funds are the distinct exception. Costs do matter—that much we can say with absolute certainty. The less you spend on management fees and other investment expenses, the more money you are going to have in your pocket at the end of the day.

So what should we keep in mind when creating an X-Factor investment model strategy? Four main things: stock market and portfolio selection is extremely important; risk management and preservation of capital is important; cash flow is important; and, needless to say, taxes are important. Remember, it's the real after-tax return that counts, having the cash flow you need to maintain the lifestyle you want through asset preservation. You can achieve this through the power of simplification: simplifying your financial plan to focus on low-risk, low-tax, low-cost investments that generate multiple streams of cash flow.

The truth is, you don't need to be in every asset category. You don't need to own 30 different mutual funds. What every investor does need is a simple, concentrated portfolio that focuses on triple-A, blue-chip investments, cost control, tax reduction, and capital preservation. That's the approach that is going to be successful in the long term.

iii. Low-risk strategies

Thanks to the recent empirical studies generated at York University's Schulich School of Business under Professor Moshe Milevsky, we can see very clearly today that risk plays a huge role in the performance of a guaranteed investment certificate, or GIC.

When most Canadians think about a GIC, they look at the word "guaranteed" and they think "no risk." They are happy to make 2.5 percent on their GICs over five years because they believe the money is guaranteed. However, if they took the time to factor in the impact of tax and inflation on their return over the term of the investment, they would find that they have no return at all. That's the risk— you are getting nothing for your money. In fact, over the course of most five-year periods during the last thirty years, the return on the average GIC investment would be negative, a loss of capital over the term of the investment.

If that same GIC was inside an insurance policy, the insurance company would pay bonus interest through the remission of premiums, thus pushing the cash flow up to, perhaps, four percent. And because the investment was inside an insurance policy, it would also be risk-free and tax-free. But that is the only way that GIC investment could have made a return for the investor today, and, obviously, that's the benefit of knowledge and good financial planning. Short of losing your entire investment, a negative return is the worst of all possible investment outcomes because the key element to consider when investing is capital preservation. For that reason, it is essential that the investor always be aware of the level of risk associated with each investment product, even if that product purports to carry no risk.

Managing risk is integral to good investment planning. For example, if you purchase an annuity (there are a number to choose from on the market: structured annuities, back-to-back annuities, etc.), it is a good idea to use two insurance companies in order to reduce the risk associated with the investment: Place the prescribed annuity—one that has a guaranteed cash flow that never goes up or down—with one insurance company, making sure to check its credit rating beforehand. The next step is to take out an insurance policy with another triple-A-rated insurance company that guarantees the return of the original capital tax-free to your estate when you die. That is a good example of an approach to investing that has a risk strategy built in.

Another investment vehicle that guarantees capital is the segregated mutual fund. Of course, there is nothing new about segregated mutual funds; they are more than 40 years old, in fact. The idea behind the segregated fund is that it is a product that is "segregated" from the insurance or mutual fund company's other assets or products, thus offering additional protection against risk. Through this product, the company then guarantees, for an additional premium, to return your original capital after, say, 10 years. The segregated fund is, therefore, an insured investment—if you put in $100,000 today, and after 10 years the investment fails to perform, the company will return $100,000 to you.

Some companies guarantee to return up to 75 percent of the original investment, but that is definitely not worth the effort. Your probability of loss over the 10 years is around 10 percent, so a 75 percent guarantee is nonsense.

The segregated mutual fund provider also guarantees that if you die during the 10-year term, it will make your estate whole. In addition, the asset is perceived to be credit-approved and it is a non-probatable asset in the estate. So you are paying a premium for a purpose, but that purpose only really benefits older investors.

This kind of investment can also sometimes make sense for individuals in high-risk professions. If you are something like a medical practitioner, a legal practitioner, or a real estate developer, you are much more likely to be sued than individuals in other jobs and professions. For this kind of at-risk investor, the segregated mutual fund can be seen as a kind of asset-protection strategy. But while segregated funds may save you from investing offshore, the question remains: is it worth paying the additional premium for that protection in the long term?

There are many risk-reduction strategies when it comes to financial planning, and employing them appropriately is the essence of risk management. In the same way you buy life insurance to protect your family from income loss, you must employ risk management strategies to protect capital. Part of that strategy involves working only with companies that have triple-A credit ratings, and here you must rely on third-party credit rating providers, such as Standard & Poors, who will attest to the financial stability of the financial service or product provider you are considering. But very few companies meet the triple-A test, which is why you should have a simplified portfolio structure.

iv. Keeping costs down

Keeping costs down is another integral part of risk management, so much so that even when employing risk management strategies, you should only incur the costs you require. There are lots of risk management products to choose from on the market today: disability insurance, long-term care insurance, critical care insurance, and term insurance, to name a few. All of these risk management products exist to protect us from the many threats to our personal and financial well-being that can occur in our lifetime. And the better the protection, the higher the premium we pay for it.

All risk management products represent a cost, but they also represent an investment. For example, if you buy a term life insurance policy for $1,000 that promises to pay your beneficiaries $250,000 in the event of your accidental death, that is a phenomenal return on your $1,000 investment if it is ever called upon. But only about three percent of term policies are ever acted upon during the prime earning years of the policy holder, meaning 97 percent of policy holders invest their money but never make a claim on their policy.

With odds like that, you might well ask if it is worth investing in term life insurance. Well, if you die accidentally we know you won't get the benefit of that money but your family will. That means you get the benefit of peace of mind for your $1,000 at the very least while you are alive. That is worth something. But, once again, just how much peace of mind is worth, and how much you can afford, comes down to an issue of cost. Remember, if you control the costs you incur, your cash flow and returns are going to be higher.

v. Keeping taxes down

Tax is also a critical consideration in any cost analysis. Everything you do with regard to your personal finances must be "tax managed." We do this by, first of all, maximizing deductions, but also by being aware of the ways in which income streams differ. For example, capital gains and dividends are taxed at a lower rate than ordinary income. Also, depending on the nature of the income you earn, you may be able to employ income management strategies like income splitting. These strategies usually involve placing income in the hands of lower-income family members.

Tax deferral strategies, meanwhile, allow us to defer paying a portion of our income tax until some time in the future when, presumably, our total income will be reduced. Ironically, however, if you do a good job of planning your retirement during your prime earning years, your income may, in fact, be as high after retirement as it was during your working life, or even higher. In a case like this, tax deferral strategies only end up creating greater tax liability down the road.

This situation was made even worse in 2000 when the government introduced four narrow tax brackets that have a particularly nasty effect on individuals who increase their income after retirement. As their income rises, as it probably would if you are drawing from a RRIF, you just about move up to a higher tax bracket with each incremental dollar.

In addition, when capital assets are placed inside registered investments like RRSPs and RRIFs, those assets, when withdrawn, are treated as regular income and taxed at the ordinary rate, rather than as capital gains, which are taxed at half the ordinary rate. Plus, capital losses inside registered investments are not tax deductible, unlike capital losses outside, which can be carried back three years and carried forward indefinitely.

In the end, the goal of all cost-control strategies is to generate maximum cash flow. We want to have the maximum tax-ameliorated cash flow we can achieve so that we can maintain the lifestyle we want both before and after retirement. Cash flow is the essential component of proper X-Factor investing; it is at the heart of financial control and the by-product of simplicity.

vi. Top four under 40

Research shows that there are a few critical things each investor should strive to achieve before the age of 40. The first among these is discharging all credit card debt. Credit card interest is non-deductible and you will never make a return on any investment that is equivalent to that interest after tax. Therefore, get rid of that debt as quickly as possible and dump the high-interest credit cards.

Second order of business for the under-40s: buy a house. Yes, you are incurring a large debt, but with record-low interest rates it is not an imprudent strategy. Plus, your principal residence is a tax-free zone that will, hopefully, appreciate in value while providing stability for yourself and your family at the same time. Instead of looking at a house as just a huge debt, you should look at it as a long-term, tax-free asset; and you can always "trade up" for a better one at any time if your financial situation improves.

Third, it is also a good idea for individuals under 40 to put some money away in a Registered Educational Savings Plan. It is a good idea because any children an individual investor has are likely going to be heading to college or university before the investor retires, setting up a potentially deep financial pothole down the road. In addition, RESP investments qualify for wonderful federal grants, especially if the investor's income is under $70,000.

Next, invest in a term life insurance policy. Term insurance is cheap and abundant; you can even buy it on the Internet. It doesn't really matter where you get it, but make sure you do, because it is the best way to ensure risk protection for your family should something happen to you, the principal wage earner.

That's it. Those are the four key considerations for the investor under 40: eliminate high-interest debt, and invest in a principal residence, RESPs, and term life insurance. And with the cash you will save by paying off the high-interest debt, and having a low, variable-rate mortgage, you will be able to invest in a triple-A, blue-chip portfolio and perhaps even start an entrepreneurial venture or a new business to generate even more cash flow.

PART 6

The Concentrated, Blue-Chip, Triple-A Portfolio

What is the best investment strategy? Every strategy has its merits and its faults, and 20 different investment experts can give you 20 differing opinions on which approach is best. In my experience, however, the most dependable approach, and the approach that lies at the heart of X-Factor investing, is a focus on blue-chip, triple-A investments.

From our empirical research into what the rich do, as well as the accumulated experience of the top investment strategists of the last century, we know that almost all high-net-worth individuals are "focus/concentration" investors. They do not believe that you need "one of each," as the diversification model suggests.

One popular form of portfolio diversification in recent years has been index investing, an approach that appeals to many casual investors mostly because of its low cost. Unfortunately, when an investor buys the market index, what they are really buying is the market valuations and price/earnings multiples of the entire market, which may or may not be in line with current reality. During the period between 2000 and 2002, the valuations most certainly were not in line, and the result was investors were buying an overvalued index. Therefore, even though the fee was low, the risk was high, and the potential for return was greatly diminished.

In addition, in most cases it is just 10 or 15 stocks that give the index most of its value. If you were one of those unfortunate TSE 300 buyers during the period when Nortel represented almost a third of the value of the index, your portfolio took a beating when Nortel dropped severely in value. Once again, low cost but high risk, because the value of the fund is concentrated in just a few very powerful stocks.

Now this is not to say there is no place for index buying. In fact, there may even be some real advantages to it in some cases because most portfolio managers will not outperform the index over time. Index buying can be a viable risk management strategy and cost reduction strategy during a time when there are low market index valuations combined with low cost. At any other time, however, index buying can actually increase risk.

What about active management? I've had many investors ask me whether or not this approach really works. It really depends on how you define active management. My definition of active management has more to do with stock selection than portfolio rotation over time. Simply put, my stock selection focus is always on companies with high cash reserves, low debt, and the ability to pay substantial dividends. History shows that there is usually a direct correlation between the dividend payer and long-term capital appreciation and long-term, after-tax return to the investor. That's really the key to selecting stocks.

i. A Buffett approach

If you were to attend Warren Buffett's annual meeting each year, you would find that his approach to investing really doesn't change that much over time. If he doesn't see good valuations in the marketplace, or if he thinks stocks are overvalued, he tends to keep his assets in cash—and in fact has record amounts sitting in cash today. Alternatively, with so much of his assets in cash, he has been doing some buying on the foreign exchange markets in anticipation of a devaluation of the American dollar.

Essentially, Mr. Buffett buys nothing but quality businesses that afford him a "margin of safety." This idea of the investor's margin of safety actually goes back to Professor Benjamin Graham of Columbia University, author of *The Intelligent Investor* and, not coincidentally, the man who taught Warren Buffett about investing. The margin of safety is an element of surplus or security associated with a given company's long-term financial stability. Professor Graham developed his theories about investment strategy throughout the 1930s, '40s, '50s, and '60s, so he knew a thing or two about investing in both stable and high-risk environments.

Therefore, if you were to take Buffett's passive management approach, paying appropriate attention to all the elements of risk, the task of stock selection really becomes a question of philosophy and, of course, performance. You can start, as we did, by taking a look at all the companies worldwide that actually qualify for the coveted triple-A credit rating. When you look into it, you will soon find that very few companies actually make the list.

In addition, we also wanted to look at companies with the largest cash reserves. Two good examples of companies with abundant reserves are Microsoft and Berkshire Hathaway, which have combined cash reserves totalling some US$70-billion. Cash on hand is an equally important element when trying to determine a company's financial stability.

Believe it or not, we could find only eight companies worldwide that met the triple-A ratings standard. The insurance giant American International Group (AIG) was actually the only company that exceeded all the triple-A ratings requirements. And if you map its performance against a useful index, such as the S&P, you will get a very good insight as to how the company performed over time.

Exxon Mobil was another company that qualified for the triple-A rating, as was General Electric. In fact, if you were to create an index of triple-A companies, General Electric would account for about 13 percent of the total value. That is overvalued from a mutual fund perspective, but if you take into account its huge cash reserves and the diversified nature of its business (high tech, low tech, investment, insurance), GE is really too big and diversified to be regarded as a single company working in one specific sector. Also, in addition to being diversified in terms of business, we found that these triple-A companies were also diversified geographically. Most operate on a truly global basis, with subsidiaries in perhaps 140 or 150 countries around the world.

So while Mr. Buffett may appear to invest in only three economic business sectors overall, through specific stock selection he is actually investing in a wide range of sectors, businesses, and regions. This is because the companies he invests in are diversified into multiple divisions operating in a number of business sectors in markets around the world.

Other companies that made our triple-A investment portfolio included Johnson & Johnson and Merck Pharmaceutical. It doesn't take an expert to see why there are a lot of bio-medical- and healthcare-related companies on our list—those are major growth sectors in the economy, especially with the demographic changes taking place in society. As well as that, these companies have lots of cash, so it's not surprising that high-net-worth individuals are heavily invested in both the bio-med and healthcare sectors—although, of late, scandals and product scares have adversely affected this sector and dramatically reduced stock prices to a point that while their credit rating was threatened they are trading at low valuations.

There were some notable exceptions to the bio-med/healthcare trend on our list of triple-A companies. One was United Parcel Service, which is certainly one company that has reaped the benefits of the Internet and the wonder of online shopping. But while parcel delivery is the top focus at UPS, the company has become much more diversified through some recent acquisitions. Automatic Data Processing, the giant payroll company, also made our list.

When we put all these triple-A-rated companies

together, we end up with a portfolio of only 10 stocks. Some differ widely in terms of their core business, but they all share two essential attributes: a triple-A credit rating and large cash reserves. Together these two elements give us the "margin of safety" that Prof. Graham and Mr. Buffett are looking for.

ii. Cash is king

There are several other factors that can be incorporated into a good stock-selection strategy. One idea that has come out of the recent research is that investors should focus less of their attention on price/earnings multiples and more on cash from operations, or CFO. The thinking here is if you divide the stock price by the CFO, you will get a much better predictor of long-term stock market performance. Also, if you compare the number you get to market indexes, companies with higher ratios of cash to stock price will tend to outperform companies with lower ratios over time.

If I was to invest in the blue-chip/triple-A portfolio we have created in a mutual fund, I would expect the MER to be under two percent. Furthermore, I would expect it to decline as the mutual fund assets increased, because there are definitely economies of scale in managing such a portfolio. Besides, as long as these companies maintained their triple-A rating, there would be no real reason for active management—therefore no taxes, no distributions, no reporting slips on capital gains transactions from the buying and selling of stock. So we have created a tax-efficient portfolio outside of a registered investment.

In addition, because these companies have large amounts of cash and dividend-paying ability, this is also an income portfolio. I would also expect that, over time, we might be able to acquire it within an insurance policy, as some insurance companies now allow some variation of this structure.

Clearly, there are huge advantages to this type of port-folio structuring. It provides what I would call a "proper" amount of diversification; as we have seen, you don't need to have 10 or 12 different stocks to have proper diversification. And if you were to integrate this type of portfolio with some asset-backed securities and some insurance products, you would have all the investments you really need, especially with life insurance and some other products to provide the cash flow you require in retirement.

Also, with a systematic withdrawal plan in place to create additional cash flow, this strategy works very effectively because you could withdraw about eight percent of your capital per year for the first six years without triggering any income tax, even though this is outside a registered investment. That means tax-free cash flow with no claw-back and no higher tax brackets to worry about.

PART 7

Safety of Capital

Why should you protect capital? It might seem like the answer to that question goes without saying. But, believe it or not, many investors still don't grasp the importance of this concept. Simply put: the protection of capital at all costs is really the essence of proper financial planning.

We need to protect capital because estate planning is an imperfect science. People make mistakes when they plan for their retirement. They assume they won't still be alive and kicking 30 years after they stop working. And they assume extraordinary rates of return of 10 percent or better on their investments that are simply not there.

Many investors like to imagine sky-high rates of return, but the fact is rates of 10 percent or higher almost always have no basis in reality; they are usually the result of data mining that amounts to little more than fiction. In fact, if you analyze real return numbers for equity mutual funds from 1950 to today, you will see that most funds average between two and six percent annually; on bond funds the average is around two percent; on money market funds, probably zero or even negative return.

When it comes to protecting capital, it is absolutely essential for every investor to have realistic expectations about the rates of return they can expect to get on their investments. The reason for this is simple enough: if you believe your investments are generating higher returns than they really are, you might also start believing that you can afford to spend more money right now while still meeting your retirement planning goals. In most cases, if someone thinks they can afford to spend money on something they want, they spend it. That kind of mindset can quickly lead to things like impulse buying, wasteful spending, and the incurring of unnecessary costs, all of which have the ability to burn up capital at an alarming rate.

Capital-protection strategies

If the protection of capital is central to your investment plan, as it should be, then the utilization of segregated mutual funds, in a limited capacity, may be worthwhile. Prescribed annuities can be another useful strategy, provided they are structured properly with guarantees of cash flow and with insurance in place to return the capital tax-free to the estate.

GICs inside tax freedom zones are also useful, and the tax efficiency of this method is extremely important. There are a number of tax freedom zones available to investors, and any investment that is tax efficient is naturally going to help protect capital. We have, for example, our principal residence; we are allowed to buy and sell one residence each year, and it is tax-free in the estate (although it is a probatable asset).

Back-to-back annuities also create a very tax-efficient cash flow and a return of capital tax-free to the estate. Registered Educational Savings Plans (RESPs), meanwhile, give a 25-year tax deferral. Also, unbeknownst to many investors, anyone can be the beneficiary of an RESP. The beneficiary doesn't get the grant from the government if they are over 17, but you can still defer tax for 25 years as the beneficiary of a plan regardless of age. Even pre-paid funerals are a tax-deferral vehicle, allowing investors to defer up to $35,000. Life insurance vehicles also represent tax freedom zones of the highest quality.

Regardless of the investment vehicle you prefer, the focus of your strategy should always remain the same: safety of capital; prevention of loss; mitigation of risk. It is for precisely this reason that you should take the triple-A, concentrated approach to investing. For one thing, it is very difficult for the average investor to monitor 30 or 40 different investments, and that is why the complex, highly diversified approach doesn't work for most people. Yet most actively managed mutual funds have between 50 and

250 stocks. If an investor was to buy six or seven funds like that, they could be looking at better than 1,000 individual stocks in their portfolio. It is just not possible to properly monitor that many stocks and do it successfully. That's why the X-Factor approach to investing, with its focus on simplification, triple-A-rated companies, and capital preservation, simply makes more sense.

PART 8

Real Estate

Real estate is the largest single asset class most Canadians own. Real estate is known as a "hard asset," along with things like oil, gas, precious metals, and commodities, as opposed to "soft" assets like cash, bonds, equities, mutual funds, and so on.

Generally, the hard asset classes have tended to run counter-cyclical to the soft asset classes. Therefore, as hard assets went up in value, financial assets tended to go down, and vice versa. This fact gave rise to the idea of investors keeping 10 to 15 percent of their holdings in hard assets as a hedge against steep declines in the financial markets. This strategy was validated in the late 1990s by Professor Roger Ibbotson of Ibbotson Associates, who published a study that said the "hard asset" strategy actually reduced overall portfolio risk by as much as 20 percent.

Although the hard and soft asset categories have tended to run counter-cyclical over time, today we appear to have the best of both worlds. Real estate values are high, as are energy and commodities prices. At the same time, 2003 was a very good year for equities (although 2004 appeared sluggish by comparison). Therefore, if you have your own principal residence and maybe some other real estate investments, you have a very good margin of safety in your overall portfolio should the equity markets take a downturn.

Real estate values do, of course, have a direct correlation with interest rates, and that makes them much easier to predict. For example, if there are 160,000 units of new condominium construction planned in a given marketplace over the next three years, and you know that that market can only absorb about 10,000 new units per year, it doesn't take a rocket scientist to figure out that condominium prices will go down.

In spite of this, we know that there are still speculators

out there who buy five, ten, or even twenty condo units at a time in the hope they will find five, ten, or twenty dumb people to sell them to down the road—this is known, appropriately enough, as "greater fool" theory. But these kinds of speculators have done abysmally in recent years because the glut in the market caught up with them. We have seen the same thing happen time and again in various markets around the country, with real estate booms and bubbles making and breaking investors.

When will the current real estate bubble burst? That is really hard to predict. It is safe to say, with all the new construction going on at the moment, mostly spurred by low interest rates, that there will be an oversupply of new housing units in some markets that will take several years to be absorbed. That means it will be harder for real estate investors to get liquidity, but real estate is not really for speculation anyway. Vacation properties, on the other hand, have done extraordinarily well as an investment category in North America over the last several years.

Generally speaking, I believe we can expect to see new investment strategies coming forward with respect to real estate. Some will involve various limited partnership structures that will allow investors to invest in a commercial or industrial development or, perhaps, a retirement residence that will generate a cash flow, some minor tax benefits, and capital gains after five to seven years. Structures like this were very attractive in the early 1990s and a lot of people made a lot of money on them.

The age gap

Your real estate needs and investment options will evolve over the course of your lifetime. Younger people, for example, usually want a single-family home, whether detached or semi-detached, where they can raise their children. And when they acquire a home like this, they really don't see it as an investment strategy in the beginning.

As people get older, however, the general perception is that they will want to "downsize" their real estate holdings. With their children grown and starting a life of their own, the thinking is that older people need less space, and will therefore opt to "trade down" to a smaller principal residence. While there is certainly some of that going on, the empirical research shows us that many people, especially those in their late 50s and early 60s, are actually buying *more* real estate as they get older. Some may still sell their principal residence, but they don't necessarily trade down; some actually purchase a newer, smaller principal residence and invest in a vacation property as well.

The truth is, regardless of our age, we all love bricks and mortar. People want more square footage, not less. And as long as that remains the case, real estate will remain a very stable investment category. So while the real estate market is not without its dangers, it definitely has a role to play in terms of financial planning. Real estate investing is here to stay, and it should definitely be a part of any X-Factor portfolio.

The New Estate Imperative

Tax-Free and Risk-Free Forever

The Challenges of Life

What's the point of having dreams and striving to make them a reality for yourself and your family if you just end up handing those dreams, or the best part of them, over to Canada Customs and Revenue in the form of tax? Creating a better life for ourselves and our children is why we live and why we work; we don't do it to create additional revenue for the government. If that's all we're working for, then why bother?

So how do we manage to create our dream life and pass it on to our children? We face many challenges in our lives today when it comes to building wealth and hanging on to it, and the world has changed dramatically in recent years. That means we have to learn, and relearn, how to manage our finances, especially during the last third of our lives, if we want to achieve our dreams.

We spend the first third of our lives going to school and learning things so we can develop a job or a profession. We spend the next third of our lives working like slaves accumulating capital, acquiring a house, raising a family, educating children, paying off debt, and putting away a few dollars for retirement. After all that hard work, the last third of our lives should be the best third of our lives, a time for fun and enjoyment spent, it is to be hoped, in good health and doing the things we love to do. The last thing we want is to spend that last third living in fear and anxiety because we are not in control of our finances.

Finances are actually the greatest single cause of family conflict, and they are the biggest problem retired Canadians face today. In fact, we are seeing large numbers of people living below the poverty line during the last 30 years of their lives in Canada today, largely because they have not prepared or planned properly for their retirement.

On the bright side, it's never too late to take control of

your finances and your life. Even though you may not have done all the things you should have done financially, and even if you are over 65, it doesn't mean that you can't change. Contrary to popular belief, you can, in fact, make significant changes to your personal financial health after the age of 60 that can affect the next 20 or 30 years.

It's true: things have changed. But it is never too late to learn new ways to adapt to our changing world and make it work for you. Once you do, you can create a financial plan that will allow you to be as tax-free, as risk-free, and as secure as possible for the rest of your life.

PART I

What Is Estate Planning?

Back in the "good ol' days," estate planning was a pretty simple process. Basically, the first thing you did was sit down with your solicitor and make out a will. In that, you specified who got grandma's watch and spelled out how you wanted your estate wrapped up when you died. After that, you probably put some powers of attorney in place in case you became unable to make financial or health decisions for yourself during your lifetime. That was it—a couple of hours at the lawyer's office and your estate planning was done.

While that approach may have worked once, it is simply not adequate to cope with today's changing world. Essentially, old estate planning was based on looking at the legalities regarding personal finances after somebody died. But the truth is, those old clichés *never* worked, because they were never really about estate planning.

I've spent many years working with large associations and groups of seniors, such as the Canadian Snowbird Association, who, you would think, would be very interested in the subject of estate planning. But after speaking to literally thousands of seniors over the years, I found that many of them were totally confused when it came to the subject of estate planning. "Well, we did a will back in 1972," one person said to me once, "what do we need to do estate planning for?" When you are faced with an attitude like that, the only way to explain estate planning in the modern sense is to start at the very beginning.

What is real estate planning? Real estate planning consists of four basic components:

    i. creating multiple income streams,
    ii. not outliving your money,
    iii. protecting capital, and
    iv. paying taxes.

i. Creating multiple income streams

The last 30 years of your life are supposed to be the most enjoyable, stress-free time that you have. You are supposed to be able to enjoy the wealth you have accumulated, continue to have good return on your investments, and in general feel safe. Unfortunately, because times have changed, it is no longer prudent to rely on just your RRIF, a pension cheque, or your Canada pension. The wise investor will look at creating other sources of retirement income.

In addition to all the traditional forms of retirement income, which are subject to taxation and claw-back, what we want to do in our estate plan is fund the last 30 years of our lives by generating multiple streams of cash flow. That means not one, not two, but possibly three or even four streams of cash flow to ensure we don't run out of money before we run out of life. This strategy is called "duration matching," and it is an important concept to understand.

We are living far longer today than we've ever lived before, plus we are staying far more active as we age. That means we are likely going to need a lot more money than previous generations needed for retirement. If you have multiple streams of income, you are obviously going to be far more secure and, depending on what kind of income streams you develop, end up paying much less tax.

There are many interesting cash flow options out there (and we will discuss them in more detail later on): annuities; systematic withdrawal plans; income trusts; insured pension plans—to name just a few. And with all these options at your disposal, there are lots of ways to create multiple income streams.

ii. Not outliving your money

Obviously, we don't want to outlive our money; that's why it is so important to keep money coming in after retirement and to hang on to the money we have. Not outliving our money means ensuring there will always be enough capital there to allow us to maintain the lifestyle and the quality of life that we want for the rest of our life—no matter how long that may be.

Nobody outlives their money on purpose, but so many things have changed in the investment environment today that many people are now, in fact, going broke in retirement. As a result, we see more and more people today living in poverty in their later years. The irony is, there is really no need for that to happen, especially when you can control your financial future today. We have been telling people for years that you can control the taxes you pay, the risk you take on in your portfolio, the costs you incur when investing (which do matter), and the cash flow you generate. If you control these controllable factors properly, you really can ensure that you don't run out of money before you run out of life.

iii. Protecting capital

The next key to financial security as you get older is learning how to protect capital at all costs, and that means avoiding risk. You cannot, after you are retired, afford to replace capital you accumulated when you were in your working years. The prospect of going back to work full-time is simply not a reasonable thing for most older people to consider, although many have had to in recent years because of enormous stock market losses.

Therefore, if your goal is to protect existing capital, then risk management becomes critical. It's for just that reason that no one under the age of 65 should ever look at a segregated mutual fund, which is a mutual fund with a capital guarantee. After 65, however, a segregated mutual fund is a useful proposition, as is the use of certain annuities that provide capital guarantees. Older investors should start to direct their capital into investment vehicles that come with an iron-clad guarantee that says, "No matter what happens, you will at least get your money back."

iv. Paying taxes

The final critical element on the modern estate planning list is paying the taxes. That means not only do you have to ensure you don't run out of money before you run out of life, you also have to ensure you are able to cover off the tax man when you do. If you want to leave anything at all to your children, other family members, or charity after you are gone, you must first figure out how to pay the estate taxes on your demise.

There are three levels of taxes in most jurisdictions that have to be paid on death. For example, when somebody dies, the province that they live in normally wants a probated will, meaning they want you to go to probate court, with Quebec being the lone exception. The fees for probate range from a low of $75 in Alberta up to as much as 1.5 percent of everything you own, including your principal residence, in the province of Ontario.

After probate fees comes capital gains tax. On the death of a taxpayer, the government says, "We deem the deceased to have sold all stocks, bonds, securities, businesses, farms, assets, and investment real estate on the day of their death, even if they didn't, and any gains made on the sale of such assets will be exposed to capital gains tax." Depending on the province you live in, that could mean anything from 19.5 percent up to almost 25 percent of the appreciated capital gain. That's a pretty big chunk of your capital.

Then we have the tax on RRSPs and RRIFs, of course. The entire amount is paid into your terminal return if there is not a spousal beneficiary, and the government can grab, depending on the province, anywhere between 39 and 49 percent of that amount.

When you add up those three columns of taxes applicable upon death, the deceased taxpayer could lose, on average, anywhere between 30 and 35 percent of their net worth to the government. That's the single most taxing experience you are ever likely to endure. Fortunately for you, however, you won't be there to see it, but those taxes have to be paid nonetheless. And that's really the last element of estate planning: making provisions to pay your estate taxes without resorting to the forced liquidation of everything you own. The best way to do this is to find a mechanism, usually insurance, that will guarantee the estate taxes can be paid upon the death of the taxpayer.

Where to start

So, where do you start to make a proper estate plan? You have to start at the very beginning, by putting aside all the clichés and outmoded thinking you have learned all these years about estate planning. When you do that, and recognize that proper estate planning means generating multiple streams of cash flow, not outliving your money, protecting existing capital, and figuring out how to pay taxes well in advance, then you will have a whole new mindset when it comes to planning for your retirement.

PART 2

An Estate Plan Is Not a Will

Everybody needs a will. The only way you could conceivably get away without having one is if you had nothing at all of value to leave behind and no real beneficiaries to leave something to anyway. Thankfully, very few people fall into that category.

Why is a will so important? A will is important mostly because financial institutions like to see a probated will before they will release assets belonging to the deceased. If you are an inheriting spouse, you probably don't need to go through the entire process; with a copy of the will, a marriage certificate, and a death certificate, you can usually get away without having to go through probate.

Upon the death of the surviving spouse, however, most provinces will force the probate process upon you. The government does this because it wants to make sure it gets the maximum tax bite, but the financial institutions are going to want to see that final piece of paper in any case. The financial institutions are very particular about seeing the will because it gets them off the hook. Basically, they want to know that they are handing over the deceased person's assets to the right party, meaning there won't be anyone suing them down the road for giving the assets to the wrong party.

However, estate planning is not a will. A will says who gets what where, how, and when after a person dies, but it doesn't spell out how the estate is to be maintained *before* death. A will may result in the establishment of various trusts, but it is not really a plan for living; it is just the final document, the final piece of the puzzle, that needs to be put in place after you have done the kind of estate planning that is going to help you maintain your wealth until your death.

But even when you have done proper estate planning

and completed a will, that doesn't mean the job is done for good. Both an estate plan and a will are dynamic tools that need to be updated on a regular basis to reflect your changing circumstances. If you understand that, you are well on the way to a happy, stress-free retirement.

PART 3

A Proper Plan for Retirement

Another important point for investors of all ages to understand is that retirement planning is actually concurrent with estate planning. By the time you start thinking about making a real retirement plan, say in your 40s or early 50s, your estate plan should already be worked out. That means the will has to be done, the insurance to pay taxes has to be in place, and the risk management concept and tax strategies have to be there; it's a concurrent strategy.

i. Underestimating longevity/overestimating returns

Unfortunately, too many people still make major mistakes when it comes to planning for their retirement. First of all, too many people grossly underestimate the amount of money they are going to need to fund the rest of their lives, largely because they have grossly underestimated their own projected longevity.

For example, it you are an adult male, aged 65, you probably want to have a financial plan in place today that will do you right through to age 90 at least. And if you are a female of the same age, a financial plan that is good to age 95 would not be unrealistic. If that seems far-fetched, consider this: in terms of actuarial science, it is assumed that a newborn child today has the potential to live as long as 105 to 110 years. I know it sounds funny to say it, but longevity is killing us financially.

Therefore, the first problem we have to tackle in terms of retirement planning is understanding that we are going to need more money than we think. Secondly, we are going to have to come to terms with the fact that we generally overestimate our ability to make major returns on our investments. In years past, retirement plans were often based on expectations of returns as high as 15 to 20 percent. This kind of hyperbolic nonsense was dreamed up in the mid-1990s when some people were getting rich off of inflated bubble markets, and we all know what happened with that. Today, those kinds of returns are simply fantasy.

If you would rather base your retirement plan on realistic returns, you should probably be thinking more in terms of six to eight percent—six if you want a safe number to work with, and eight if you are a lot more optimistic and a lot younger.

Therefore, if you were sitting down to do a proper retirement plan today, you would start with a realistic expectation of investment returns of about six percent. Second, you would expect your retirement years to last somewhere in the region of 30 years, from 65 to 95.

In a survey by MetLife, people were asked to estimate the chances that a 65-year-old today would live beyond the age of 85. More than 60% placed the odds at about 25%.

However, current statistics suggest that, on average, a 65-year-old today has a 50% chance of living beyond their 85th birthday.

And finally, because we have consistently underestimated the amount of money we are going to spend over the course of those 30 years, you should be planning to save much more than you plan to spend. After retirement, you can expect to start withdrawing money at a rate of eight to twelve percent of your total capital annually. Therefore, if you don't want to run out of money, you are going to have to either withdraw less after you retire or save a lot more beforehand.

ii. Ignore the clichés

It seems like a vicious cycle, but the sad truth is, too many people are their own worst enemy when it comes to retirement planning. They spend too much time listening to the clichés and buying into the hype that the investment industry puts forward. One of the big clichés that many investors have bought into over the years is the notion of saving 10 percent of your income for retirement. Well, the truth is you can't build assets by saving just 10 percent annually. If you want to build adequate, long-term wealth, given reasonable longevity, the savings rate has got to be much higher: 15 or even 20 percent per year if at all possible.

Another cliché the financial planning industry likes to trumpet is the idea of investment diversification. The problem is, most diversification strategies offered up by the industry don't make any sense. In fact, most global markets involve so much risk that they are not really worthwhile for the average investor. The fact is, most of the investment concepts and strategies that were the "be-all and end-all" in the mid-1990s never really worked. On top of that, many investors today find themselves still bound by the mistakes they made a decade ago because they have ignored all the changes that have taken place with regard to tax law.

What's the bottom line? It's simple:

- forget the clichés of the past;

- expect to live in retirement for at least 30 years;

- you are probably not going to do much better than six percent return on your investments, although you will need a lot more; and

- you should plan to save a lot more money than you are going to need.

Just do the math: if you have to live on 50 or 60 percent of the average of your best five years' salary for the duration of your retirement, you are going to be living at a very low level relative to what you are used to. But you are going to want to be active after you retire, you will want to travel and do things, so you better plan to have enough money to do it all.

iii. Pay attention to the rule changes

There have been a lot of tax rule changes in recent years that directly impact your ability to formulate an effective retirement plan.

Interest deductibility

Interest deductibility, for example, may not be available in the long term, as the government moves away from that because people are just not making real absolute returns. The government doesn't like to see investors borrowing money at five percent and then getting a dividend at one-and-a-half percent; they don't like investors to create losses. I think we can expect to see changes there in the not-too-distant future.

Income trusts

The government has also changed the rules governing income trusts. First of all, pensions may not be allowed to have more than a few percent of their assets invested in one of the business trusts, which greatly reduces their potential investment returns. Secondly, from now on on your T3 reporting slips you are going to get a report on the return of capital, meaning when that capital is returned when you sell your income trust you are going to have a huge capital gains liability. Once again, the government is looking to tax, and tax, and tax again.

Gifts-in-kind

On December 5, 2003, the very attractive, multi-year benefit called the "Gifts-in-Kind Donation Plan" was eliminated in the federal budget. That was a strategy where you could put up $1,000, get a receipt for fair market value of $5,000, and get $2,400 back in tax credits. So even with capital gains you got back 50 to 60 percent of your original investment. When the government killed that program, it was just one more tax-reduction strategy gone.

(But not for rich people, of course; they can still use this strategy if they are doing something like donating collectible art or expensive real estate or environmental land.)

RRSPs

We have also seen a number of major rule changes when it comes to RRSPs, and the most onerous of these has been the claw-back tax. The first RRSP claw-back taxes actually came in in 1989. Then in 1997, Mr. Martin, the Finance Minister at that time, started to go after RRSP money in earnest by targeting senior citizens specifically. Many of the Canadian Snowbirds I would meet attending seminars over the years would often tell me, "Gee, I just got hit with another $12,000 in taxes now that I've got RRIF income." That's a perfect example of claw-back taxes in action, and they can add up to a big loss of capital for you.

If, for example, you are over 65 years of age and your income exceeds $27,000 a year, the government will claw back your age tax credit. On top of that, in 2000 the government introduced four narrow tax brackets. So now when you roll to a RRIF you are more than likely going to be bumped to a higher bracket and end up paying more tax on every incremental dollar. Then, if you add the provincial rate on top of the federal rate, you add insult to injury.

Clearly, tax rules that target retirement savings are a major problem for every Canadian. In fact, the C.D. Howe Institute has put out several reports in recent years that draw a direct connection between RRSP ownership and poverty among seniors. Although most people are completely unaware of this research, it clearly shows that if you have less than $100,000 in an RRSP you are better off melting it down gradually and getting the money out because government benefits after retirement are equivalent to about $250,000 in an RRSP, but without all the punitive taxes and claw-backs.

The claw-back tax is a 15 percent tax on top of your

top rate if your aggregate income exceeds $60,000 a year. Aggregate income would include the gross up on Canadian dividends combined with capital gains, but with none of the credits or deductions included. So any way you look at it, it's a pretty mean-spirited tax, especially when you consider that it was specifically designed to claw back Old Age Security.

In addition, it is also important to remember that on the death of a taxpayer who does not have a spousal beneficiary, the full value of the RRSP or RRIF is paid into the terminal return, which is the return filed by your estate when you die. The government is then free to take its chunk, often as much as 49 percent depending on the province.

Remember too that many people flowed equity mutual funds into the body of their RRSPs or RRIFs during the boom times of the late 1990s and early 2000s, only to discover that their capital losses are not tax deductible—or deductible against anything for that matter. However, when you take capital gains out of an RRSP or RRIF, it is taxed at the ordinary high rate, not at the lower capital gains rate.

Considering all the potential for capital loss, it's not surprising that more and more people are starting to look at RRSPs and RRIFs not as ideal tax deferment vehicles, but more like gigantic, cumulative tax traps that do more to benefit governments in the long term. For many years, people had an almost paranoid obsession with locking money away in their RRSP every year. But today, when you factor in the aggregate impact of all the rule changes that have taken place over the years, the RRSP/RRIF is no longer the "silver bullet" retirement strategy it once was. True, it was wonderful up to a certain point in time, probably the best retirement planning strategy available for the average investor, but too many things have changed since then.

Today, the meltdown strategy may well be the best option for many investors—and that means "melting down," not "collapsing" your RRSP or RRIF. Once you have achieved that, you can start to focus your attention on where you can put your money to keep it in those protected categories we like to call "tax freedom zones," where you are able to grow capital on a tax-deferred or largely tax-free basis.

PART 4

The New Investment Environment

It only stands to reason that if a lot of things have changed in the financial planning environment, you need to have a new financial planning strategy to deal with that change. That plan starts with clearly defining the changes that have taken place. Once you can clearly see how the landscape has shifted for Canadian investors, you will get a better understanding of the necessity of formulating a new financial plan and be better motivated to take action.

i. Environmental factors—new technology/security

How has the financial planning landscape changed? Well, just look around you. Look at the new technology we have today: wireless Internet devices; plasma TVs; camera cell phones. These things were still the stuff of science fiction for the average person even 10 years ago. Fifteen and twenty years ago they were unimaginable. Our new technological world is full of both new opportunities and new challenges for investors, and this new wired reality must be taken into consideration by investors.

Another new environmental factor investors must consider today is the war on terror. Whether we know it or not, the war on terror touches all of our lives through things like higher security costs, higher taxes, and more government regulations. Security was not at the forefront of our thinking even a few years ago, but it is a critical issue today.

ii. Economic factors—inflation and interest rates

Next, look at the economic factors. Inflation, which was a huge concern at one time, is practically nonexistent today. Right now, inflation rates are hovering at around 1.8 to 2.1 percent. They may go up due to rising energy costs, but, generally speaking, there is no real threat of a massive jump in the inflation rate. For the most part, this is because the main cause of inflation in the past, government spending, has been curtailed in recent years at both the federal and provincial levels. While it's true that governments in Canada are still spending taxpayer money at a high rate, they are no longer racking up the standard 10 percent per year increases they used to. Currently, government spending increases are running in the five to six percent per year range, making them less of an inflationary factor.

And speaking of non-factors in the economy, there is no better example right now than interest rates. The last few years have seen interest rates drop to 40-year lows. That has been a boon for the housing and real estate businesses, of course, because it has allowed many more people to take out a mortgage and invest in their own home. On the other hand, record-low interest rates have also meant that fixed-income securities, a basic component of any retirement investment strategy, have lost their appeal. With very low interest rates, you simply can't make money on a savings bond, or for that matter a GIC, unless it's in a tax-sheltered structure like, say, universal life insurance (which we will discuss in more detail later).

iii. Pensions

You should also take some time to consider the evolving nature of the Canada Pension Plan and pensions in general. The government changed pension contributions so that the combined employer/employee contribution rose to 9.9 percent. The net result of this change, actuarially speaking, is that, as of 2004, the Canada Pension Plan was fully funded for the first time for the next 75 years. So unless there are huge unforeseeable upheavals in the economy, resulting in massive market and investor losses, your CPP is absolutely secure. There is no question about it; you can rest easy on that score at least.

On the other hand, one area that is not so safe, as

mentioned previously, is the area of private, or company pensions. The latest actuarial tables show us that many defined benefit pensions are clearly underfunded due primarily to market losses after the high-tech bubble burst. Too many pension fund managers got caught up in the "New Economy" hype and, as the saying goes, blew their brains out—too bad it wasn't *their* pension money they lost.

Another factor that is having a major impact on pension plans, as well as the whole financial planning process, is our changing longevity. The lifespan of Canadians has expanded dramatically over the last few decades, and because we are living so much longer, we now have to plan for our financial future using an entirely different life model. Unfortunately, many company pension plans were set up when longevity was not what it is today.

Today it is not uncommon to see defined pension shortfalls, depending on the company, of between 15 and 25 percent. Those shortfalls must be made up out of corporate profits. Unfortunately, there are also many insolvency cases where the company has gone out of business and will simply never be able to make up its pension shortfall, meaning those pension plan members are going to see their benefits cut off.

If you are enrolled in a company pension plan, you should make sure you regularly review the status of your benefits so you are not caught by surprise. Many plans are moving to reduce benefits or even convert from a "defined benefit" structure to something called a "money purchase plan," which involves significant cost increases to the members.

iv. Currency and the equity markets

Other areas where we have seen significant change are in the equity markets and the Canadian dollar.

The equity markets had a good year in 2003 and a

moderate one in 2004, but most recently we have seen a good deal of pull-back in spite of the fact company profits are up. In general, it is fair to say that the equity markets are, at best, highly volatile and very risky. The very essence of the industry was to suck you in to "the cult of equities." At one point, the endless clichés being spouted by the investment industry would have you believing that equities were absolutely the only option out there in the market-place if you wanted to build long-term value. The significant risk was worth it, the thinking went, because the returns could be so spectacular. But the losses were just as spectacular, which is a little point they usually forgot to mention.

The financial institutions love the equity markets because they never lose. Regardless of whether or not the market goes up or down, the financial institutions just continue to turn your money into their money through transaction and management fees. Actually, common sense dictates that the best equity to own is probably the financial institution you are investing with, since their stock price combined with their dividends is probably better than any product they have to offer. The same goes for mutual fund companies; you are usually better off owning the company stock than owning any of its mutual funds.

The bottom line is, equity markets have clearly been oversold to the consumer. On top of that, consumers have overexposed themselves to things they don't understand. They have bought too many stocks and too many funds, and they have not taken the time to simplify, concentrate, and focus their portfolio.

As for the Canadian dollar, we have seen it rise steadily in value for some time relative to its U.S. counterpart, but what we have seen is really an illusion. The Canadian dollar has not really been going up in value at all; it is the U.S. dollar that has been coming down. The U.S. dollar has actually been undergoing a deliberate program of devaluation for some time as part of strategy to put the greenback in a better position due to the huge trade imbalance that exists between the U.S. and its trading partners.

While a weaker U.S. dollar might be a positive thing for the American economy, a stronger Canadian dollar has been anything but positive for Canada's economy. The stronger Loonie has had a significant impact on tourism, manufacturing, and exports in Canada, as well as on Canadian investment portfolios that were heavily invested in American stocks. The dollar issue promises to remain a factor for investors for some time, which should be good news for Canadian Snowbirds at least.

v. Insurance

In case you didn't notice, the cost of insurance is going up. Property and casualty insurance rates have risen, as have rates for home and car insurance, in some cases by as much as 30 or 40 percent in recent years. That is an increased cost for everyone, regardless of age, and it is a cost that is going to follow you into retirement as well. Happily, though, some life insurance costs have gone down, though not enough to offset the increases in other areas.

You can't avoid insurance, so you had better be aware of the changes taking place in that industry.

vi. Real estate

When you are talking about the changing financial planning environment, you have to talk at some point about real estate. Thanks to record-low interest rates, real estate has been the best performing investment category for the last half-dozen years, and the corresponding increase in property values has given many seniors a degree of financial security they would never have had otherwise.

But even though much of their net worth may be locked up in their real estate holdings, seniors should avoid getting sucked in by the "reverse mortgage" nonsense that is being peddled these days; reverse mortgages are good for the financial institutions but bad for you.

If you really want to make the most of your real estate wealth, the best approach would be to downsize your housing and invest some of that equity in guaranteed secure investment vehicles that will give you good after-tax cash flow, which is really what you are after in your retirement years.

When is the best time to convert your real estate holdings to cash you can then re-invest? Basically, you have to keep your eye on interest rates. The rule of thumb in real estate is, for every one percent rise in interest rates, 10 percent of potential home buyers are eliminated from the market. So if interest rates were to rise two percent over the next two years, that means 20 percent of potential buyers will be eliminated from the market, and house prices will likely fall. Therefore, if you are over 65 years old and the value of your house has increased by 300 percent in the last 10 years in a major market, you should, by all means, consider downsizing that real estate and reinvesting your tax-free equity. Most major Canadian markets are grossly overbuilt in condos at the moment, so you should be able to get a good deal on a smaller place and still have lots of cash left over.

vii. Tax factors

Finally, there is the changing tax environment. At the federal level, we know the government has been attacking every tax reduction strategy they can find for some time, but things have been changing at the provincial level as well. Most provinces, with the exception of Alberta, have moved to raise taxes in recent years; either that, or they have done the next best thing by charging higher user fees for government services, which are just more taxes in all but name.

Meanwhile, municipal taxes have been going up as

well, because they are tied to market value assessment and property values have been going up. On top of that, the municipalities have seen the money they receive from the provincial and federal governments dwindling steadily down, so they have been looking for ways to increase revenue as well. The bottom line is, everyone is looking for more of your money.

viii. The changing investment marketplace

Believe it or not, Canadians now have a confusing array of some 6,000 different investment products to choose from. Just 10 years ago there were only about 1,500 investment products out there, and even then most investors were overwhelmed. The average investor wouldn't know where to begin with 6,000 items to choose from; that's 6,000 separate options, many of which are virtually the same; 6,000 sales pitches to decipher; 6,000 opportunities to make a mistake.

But while sifting through all those different investment choices might seem impossible, there is a way out. In the face of such a daunting task, the wise investor can always fall back on the power of simplicity. Just keep the key rules in mind: as we get older, we should own less and be more focused and concentrated with an emphasis on capital protection, tax reduction, and cash flow generation. You don't need "one of each" to get there; you don't need 20-odd mutual funds, 50-plus stocks, 100-plus income trusts. Remember, less can produce more, with lower risk, less cost, less tax, and better returns.

It is also important when making your investment choices to remember that there has been a lot of financial industry consolidation, with mutual fund companies buying up mutual fund dealers, and so on. That consolidation does not always work out to your benefit, as fewer and fewer companies means less and less competition within the industry and, therefore, higher costs to you. Inevitably, consolidations mean service will suffer, you will pay more for it, and your financial advisor will no longer be independent.

ix. A new strategy

Given all the environmental changes we have to consider today when it comes to personal finances and investing, it should be obvious that a new strategy is required to address them. We must now take into account all these factors when planning the last 30 years of our lives in order to protect our financial well-being. Change has become the only permanent part of the financial planning landscape, and the investors who do the best job of managing that change are going to be the ones who come out on top over the course of the coming years and decades.

PART 5

Cash Flow Management

For the better part of the last 30 years, the main focus of the financial planning industry has been to separate you from your money. They did it by selling you clichés—top fund, hot fund, the right bond, the right mutual fund. They did it by selling you strategies—market timing, stock picking, sector rotating, momentum playing. But no matter how they did it, the goal of every marketing slogan and sales pitch was to turn *your* cash into *their* cash. We know now—or at least we *should* know—that all of this stuff was just drivel; none of it produced any real value for investors in the long term. But now, putting all those shop-worn clichés aside, you can start your financial planning all over again, and the best place to start is with proper cash flow/risk management.

i. Delayed retirement

When it comes to cash flow and risk management, there are a number of good options to consider. Unfortunately, because of the huge losses many investors took after the collapse of the high-tech bubble, quite a few of you are simply going to have to work a lot longer than you ever thought you would have to. In fact, the most recent investor surveys have found that most people believe they are going to have to work between three and eight years longer than they originally planned. In short, they are going to have to delay retirement.

As if the prospect of working longer weren't bad enough, you can expect the government to make changes in the not-too-distant future that will restrict you from drawing down your CPP for a few more years. The U.S. government has already done this with social security, pushing eligibility for that back to age 67.

Actually, working longer is not entirely a bad idea. It

improves your cash flow, of course, but it also keeps both your body and mind active, which improves your overall health. Plus, having that extra cash later in life gives you more options for financial planning: you could set up a home-based business; you could do consulting work; you could turn a hobby into some kind of profit-making venture. Best of all, making money later in life means you don't have to encroach so much on your basic capital.

ii. Systematic withdrawal plans

There are other sources of cash flow for the retiree that don't involve working. For example, if you have a portfolio of mutual funds outside your RRSP/RRIF, you can establish a systematic withdrawal plan. Just tell your financial advisor that you would like to have a "regularized cash flow" from your investments and they can advise you how to set it up. Most of these plans can be set up such that you can withdraw money from your base capital on a regular basis at a rate of about eight percent a year for six years. And for those six years you can withdraw that money without paying a nickel in income tax because it is considered a remission, or a return, of your original capital. After that period, however, there would be some tax to pay. You would have to pay some capital gains, for example, if you were fortunate enough to make money; but even then, it would not be that much. Regardless, systematic withdrawal is still a good cash flow strategy. And remember, most mutual funds will let you withdraw up to 10 percent of your investment annually without the horrid "deferred sales" charge.

iii. Annuities

Another cash flow vehicle to consider is annuities. With interest rates at record-low levels, you are probably thinking annuities are not a good strategy, but prescribed annuities may be an exception to this rule. This type of annuity does two things: first, the capital is prescribed, meaning you get a regularized payment that will never be diminished; and second, when you pass away, whatever you put in today will come back to your estate on a tax-free basis.

Imagine, for example, you are 70 years old and you put $100,000 into a prescribed annuity. You use one financial services company as the annuity holder guaranteeing the payment, and another company to provide the insurance contract that guarantees the return of the capital to your estate on your demise. That $100,000 investment will give you an after-tax cash flow of somewhere between seven and eight percent—and for after-tax cash flow, that's pretty good. Even in its totality, most of that cash flow is not taxable in any case because it is considered a return of capital.

So, with this prescribed annuity strategy, known as a "back-to-back" annuity, you get the benefit of the regularized cash flow, plus your original $100,000 investment is returned tax-free to your estate from the insurance policy should anything happen to you. That means the asset will not be exposed to any taxes in the estate, plus it is a non-probatable asset, making it a very effective cash flow and tax reduction strategy at the same time. (If you like to use the industry jargon just to see the stunned look in your financial advisor's eyes, a prescribed annuity with an insurance guarantee is also called a "mortality swap.")

iv. Insured pension plans

Another cash flow option is to utilize insured pension plans. We know we can get a certain level of cash flow from income trusts because part of that cash flow is a return of capital, but all that strategy does is defer the tax. When you sell that income trust, anything you receive as a capital payment is deducted from the base amount; that means you have a much higher adjusted cost base, which means you will pay a lot more capital gains tax.

The same thing goes for investment real estate. The

problem with this vehicle is that the capital cost allowance write-off is essentially a tax deferral. When you sell investment real estate, you are required to take the whole amount you have written off back into income—it's called a "recapture"—and then pay tax on that total amount. So all you have done is defer the tax on that investment property until you sell it, and then you get your huge tax hit.

On the other hand, insured pension plans have been an effective cash flow strategy since January of 1982. This strategy involves the use of universal life insurance. Universal life insurance is a very effective tax and estate planning vehicle, and yet it is not really that well known by most Canadians. In our research on high-net-worth individuals, we found that about 75 percent of wealthy Canadians are users of insurance products, especially universal life insurance or variations thereof. In addition, we found that only about seven percent of middle-income Canadians have properly utilized a universal life insurance strategy.

Universal life insurance consists of two basic products. The first of these is an insurance product to pay the taxes on your demise. The reason you buy life insurance, the term insurance component of universal life insurance, is that on your demise you have, in effect, pre-paid your taxes. So, for example, if you are a 65-year-old married person now and expect to live another 30 years, given your current assets, a normal rate of withdrawal, and normal growth in your portfolio over that time frame you may end up owing perhaps as much as $500,000 in taxes upon the death of the last taxpayer. What you do, essentially, when you buy universal life insurance is make provision to pay those taxes today by making a deal with the insurance company to provide your estate with $500,000 tax-free dollars when the last spouse dies.

It is best to do this, if possible, as a couple on a last-to-die basis, because it greatly reduces the cost of the insurance. The insurance company is happy to offer this service at a reasonable rate because it does not have to pay on the policy until the last individual dies, meaning the insurance company has the use of the money for that much longer. Therefore, a 45-year-old couple would be paying the same premium on a joint and last-to-die policy that a 33-year-old individual would pay on a single life policy. Likewise, a 65-year-old couple in good health would be treated as a 55- or 56-year-old individual. So for a couple, this approach both lowers the cost of insurance and provides a tax strategy at the same time. For a single individual it is a bit more expensive, but the strategy still guarantees that their taxes will be pre-paid at the time of their death.

Of course, that $500,000 is going to cost you from 10 to 20 percent of that amount to insure over the next few years. But even if both members of the couple died the day after they made the first payment on the policy, the insurance company would still have to provide the full $500,000 to the estate; that's the way insurance works. That's half a million tax-free, non-probatable dollars made available to your estate to discharge your tax liability.

As if that wasn't incentive enough, once you create your universal life insurance strategy, you will automatically gain access to Sections 148.1, .2, .3, and .6 of the Income Tax Act, which is also known as "Maximum Taxable Actuarial Reserve" (MTAR). These sections of the Tax Act allow you to shelter, inside the insurance policy, hundreds of thousands, if not millions, of dollars from taxation for the rest of your life. Most provinces do have a small premium tax, but, generally speaking, most of the money in your insurance policy can grow tax-deferred till the day you die. Then, after your death, it can all come out tax- and probate-free and go to anyone you want anywhere in the world.

At the same time, if you find you need access to the capital that is inside the policy at any time, you can have that too. A mere 90 days after the policy is established, the insurance company will allow you to use what you have in your investment account as collateral to borrow money from a lending institution. The subsequent loan is therefore guaranteed by the funds in your account and is discharged at the time of your death by the insurance company, along with any accrued interest. Usually, the insurance company will give you access to between 75 and 90 percent of what you have in your investment account inside the policy, depending on the investment components involved.

By doing this, you create an insured pension that gives you a regular cash flow as you need it. You can take the money as a lump sum, or you can arrange to take monthly payments. Regardless of how you take the money though, it does not qualify as taxable income because it is borrowed money. Therefore, an insured pension is really tax-free cash flow that is not subject to pension claw-back tax and will not push you into a higher tax bracket. When it comes to cash flow management, it is hard to find a more effective strategy than that.

PART 6
Seniors' Taxes

Another primary objective of retirement planning is to lessen, as much as possible, the impact of seniors' taxes. I call them seniors' taxes because these taxes are particularly onerous to people over the age of 65. They include things like the loss of the age tax credit; the so-called OAS claw-back taxes; and the higher tax brackets that come into play when your retirement income exceeds the various levels in the four narrow tax brackets.

If you do proper tax planning, you should be able to cut costs, improve cash flow, and enhance your returns, but you are going to have to address the issue of seniors' taxes at some point in your life. One way you can do this is to review where you have placed your money and make sure that these vehicles don't put you into a position where you are going to generate those claw-backs.

Depending on your assets and your tax situation, one thing you might want to do around age 65 is to look at your RRSP and consider beginning to melt it down. That doesn't mean you march into your financial institution on the morning of your 65th birthday and say, "Give me all my money out of my RRSP." If you try that, you are going to get hit with a pretty large tax bill; for starters, there is a 30 percent withholding tax on any large withdrawal from a registered savings plan. No, there are ways to gradually take down an RRSP that don't involve totally collapsing it overnight.

Essentially what you are going to do is gradually withdraw the money from your RRSP in increments of $5,000. If you withdraw the money in $5,000 increments, the institution will remit 90 percent to you and withhold 10 percent for the government, meaning you get $4,500 and the government gets $500. You can do that as often as you wish: ten times a day; one day a week; one day a month. If you have $100,000 in your plan, you could make 20 systematic withdrawals over the course of 20 months and end up with $90,000.

Once you have your money out of the registered plan, you can go about creating a tax strategy that both mitigates risk and reduces tax. One way to do that is to create a number of tax deductions, strategies such as interest deductions for business loans, tax-limited partnerships, and flow-through shares, which are designed to reduce your overall taxable income. The law permits you to tax-plan down to an "alternative minimum tax" plateau of $40,000 (as of this writing). That means, that $100,000 from your RRSP meltdown that was fully taxable in your income this year can be tax-planned down to $40,000. You can further shelter $30,000 out of that $40,000 using a structured giving strategy called a leveraged, or profitable, donation (which we will discuss in more detail later).

If done properly, you will end up paying tax on just $10,000 of the original $100,000 you withdrew from your RRSP. But you already paid $10,000 in withholding tax when you took the money out, and since you will only end up owing $3,000 or $4,000 in income tax anyway, you may even end up getting a refund. The net result is going to be somewhere in the region of 96 cents on the dollar back in your pocket, where it belongs.

So what do you do with that money once you get it out of your RRSP? Well, what you are *not* going to do is put it right back into a taxable environment; if you are going to do that, you might as well just hand it right back to the bank teller when you withdraw it. Instead, you are going to relocate that money into one of a number of "tax zones" where you can get a more efficient cash flow while paying a lot less tax.

I believe we should each do everything in our power to avoid the problem of seniors' taxes, and you shouldn't feel at all guilty when you do. Taxes targeted at retirement income are totally ageist and discriminatory and they produce a whole series of punitive results for people over the age of 65. Not only that, but they punish frugality, discipline, and personal responsibility, and you deserve better than that.

PART 7

Risk Management

As we get older, we face a growing potential for the loss of capital. That risk is there, of course, throughout our lives, but life risk and capital risk are different things.

Life risk, and lifestyle risk, would include things like developing critical illnesses such as cancer and diabetes. You can buy critical illness insurance to protect your family from the loss of capital due to something like that happening. In fact, if you buy critical illness insurance when you are 50, and you remain free of that kind of illness until you reach age 65, you can usually get a full refund on your premiums, but you can't really do it after age 65.

Temporary or permanent disability is another lifestyle risk that should be addressed. During the prime earning years, the probability of disability occurring is about five times as likely as sudden death occurring, so disability insurance can be a very prudent risk management strategy. This is especially true for self-employed people and high-income earners.

Obviously, sudden death is another life risk you should factor into your risk management strategy, and basic term life insurance is the optimum strategy here. For someone under the age of 40, the critical concerns are usually paying off high-interest credit card debt, paying off the mortgage on your house, and putting an RESP in place to save for your kids' education. All of these things are in jeopardy if the prime wage earner in the family is suddenly taken away. Term insurance is there to guarantee these essential things get done even if you die suddenly.

Another risk factor to consider is long-term care. If you ever end up in a long-term care facility at some point in your life, you will find it can gobble up capital at a breathtaking rate. Also, if you want to have some quality of life in this kind of facility, you are probably looking at something in the range of $4,000 to $5,000 a month—that's a lot of money for most people. Of course, you can always resort to a government facility if you don't have that kind of money, but the waiting lists are quite long to get in to those places and the level of care is probably not what you would prefer. The beauty of long-term care insurance is that the policy kicks in to cover at least a part of the cost so that you don't end up eating through your capital as quickly as you would if you were uninsured.

When it comes to mitigating tax risk, the elements of universal life insurance are there to ensure your tax liability is covered on your demise. Segregated funds can also provide you with capital insurance and further mitigate risk. In addition, prescribed annuities and similar structures can also be highly beneficial in terms of risk management, providing truly tax-efficient capital protection. On top of that, the returns are probably as much as four times the cash flow you would otherwise get from today's fixed-income products.

Risk management strategies are there to protect us from more than the mere loss of capital. They are there to protect and guarantee a level of comfort and a lifestyle that we have managed to create for ourselves and our family and want to maintain regardless of what life throws at us along the way. There are many effective approaches—some individuals may prefer asset-backed or mortgage-backed securities; others may opt for hedge funds (which are not the same as mutual funds). But anything and everything can be a good risk management strategy so long as it protects capital and protects the lifestyle you want to maintain.

PART 8

Legal Structures

It is essential when you embark on any long-term planning exercise that you have a firm grasp of the legalities involved.

We have already talked at length about wills and powers of attorney. The will, of course, is really the final summary of your estate plan, and powers of attorney are vital when you are talking about issues like long-term disability and cases where you are unable to make financial and medical decisions for yourself. In a case like that, you would obviously prefer to have a person of your choosing making the decisions, rather than the government. In addition to wills and powers of attorney, however, there are a number of other options to consider when it comes to the legalities of financial and estate planning.

One of these options, for example, is to establish an investment holding company. If you have substantial assets—say, in excess of $250,000 in stocks, bonds, real estate—you can transfer those assets into a corporate structure. Once your estate becomes a corporation, the transfer of assets in is tax-free—this is called a "Section 85 Rollover," after the applicable section in the Income Tax Act. As the owner of your estate, you control all the voting common shares in the new corporate structure, so you control everything until the day you die. In addition to that, family members are allowed to own the non-voting preferred shares.

The goal of this strategy is to grow your capital within the corporation without exposing yourself to increased tax risk, and it does this by effecting something called an "estate freeze." From the moment of the transfer of your assets into the corporate structure until your death, all of the wealth accumulated by your investment holdings will accrue to the preferred shareholders, so you effectively freeze the value of your estate at the time of rollover. Therefore, because your assets never grow in value outside the corporation, you now know exactly how much tax liability you will have at the time of your death, and can plan accordingly.

It is also important to remember that you can "gift" assets. You can give a gift of cash to anyone you want who is over the age of 18. (If you gift cash to a minor and it is invested, all the income is attributed to you unless it is a capital gain, and then there is a whole list of other tax regulations related to that.) But if you gift stocks, bonds, securities, or investment real estate to a family member, the act of gifting is considered an act of sale, or "deemed disposition," and you will trigger a capital gain on the transaction. So if you think you are going to hand that beautiful cottage property over to your kids without paying tax on it, you can forget that.

So while capital assets are a problem, we can gift cash, and that is an important fact to know. If you want to liquidate capital assets in order to do this, that's up to you. But if you decide you would like to gift cash, it is important that you do it before your demise.

There is also a legal structure out there called a "trust" that can be beneficial in some cases. A trust is a personally binding legal structure that can be established for a certain amount of time. There are a number of trusts that can be established specifically for the purpose of the estate that allow for certain types of estate planning benefits that can really make a significant difference when it comes to the protection of capital.

You can establish a trust in your will, for example, called a testamentary trust. When assets are transferred to a spouse upon the death of a married individual, the tax on any capital gain from the deemed sale of those assets up to the date of death is paid on the deceased's final tax return. But if those assets are transferred into the testamentary trust as a spousal rollover, the capital gains taxes can be deferred until the death of the surviving spouse, just as if the assets had been left outright to that spouse.

The testamentary trust only comes into being on your death, and you can establish a number of testamentary trusts in a single will. Income earned and held in a testamentary trust is taxed at the graduated income rates as if it were a regular taxpayer, so there is no great tax advantage there, plus the trust cannot claim personal tax credits or any other refundable credits.

It is also possible to establish a living trust, also called an "inter vivos" trust, which is only in force while you are alive, but tax rules for living trusts are not as favourable today as they were some time ago. First of all, if you transfer assets into this kind of trust, there is a deemed disposition, or sale. Then, if the value of the assets increases in the trust, there is a potential capital gain liability.

The government changed the rules governing inter vivos trusts because lots of people started using them for income splitting with other family members. This created a problem of income attribution, especially with regard to people under the age of 18, so the feds cracked down on it somewhat. Now all inter vivos trusts must pay tax based on a December 31 year-end, for example. So while these living trusts are no longer as attractive a strategy as they once were, many people still look to them as a possible tax-deferment option while they are alive.

For the last few years the government has also permitted the creation of something called the "alter ego" or "joint spousal" trust. This kind of trust is also set up while you are alive and it is taxed on a unique basis. Assets transferred into a trust while you are alive are normally deemed as sold and could trigger a capital gain on their disposition as they are transferred in, usually at the top marginal tax rate. However, if you are over 65 and transfer assets into an alter ego or joint spousal trust, the transaction can be completed on a tax-free basis. You would retain the use of the assets while you are alive and you would still be responsible for paying tax on all the income earned by the assets in the trust. Upon your death, however, the assets in the trust are distributed to your beneficiaries according to the trust agreement, rather than your will. This has the effect of reducing the probatable assets in your will, and thus the cost of probate.

A joint spousal trust is similar to an alter ego trust, except you and your spouse can receive capital from the trust and defer the final tax bill on the remaining profits until the death of the last taxpayer. In order for this kind of trust to be in effect—and this is one of the more effective strategies for older people with sizeable assets—the person transferring the assets into the trust must be over 65; the trust must have been set up after 1999; all income from the trust must be paid out to the transferor during their lifetime (and no other person can receive income or capital from the trust except you or your spouse). Upon the death of the transferor, the assets in the trust must be disposed of at fair market value, but the assets are only fully taxed upon the death of the last spouse. Once again, this strategy eliminates probate fees.

Clearly, trusts and other legal structures do have certain useful applications that can be of some benefit to specific investors. But these legal structures are not strategies that any investor should jump into overnight. There is some obvious complexity here, and it is best to sit down with your financial advisor and your lawyer first to determine whether or not it is worth your while to set one or more of these structures up just to avoid probate fees. You can end up spending $3,000 or $4,000 in an effort to protect your estate from a probate fee that may only end up being around $2,000.

Finally, when it comes to your principal residence, don't even think about trying to lock that asset up in some complex legal structure. Many people think that they can avoid probate taxes by putting one of their children on title for their principal residence, but that strategy just doesn't do anybody any good. First of all, if you simply put your child on title for your principal residence they are going to have big tax problems if they try to sell your house after you die. Because they didn't pay fair market value for your house, they have no "cost base" on which to claim it as their principal residence. And if they own a separate property that they claim as a principal residence, they are going to pay huge capital gains tax on the sale of your house.

If that's not disincentive enough, what happens if your child is on title for your home and he or she gets divorced? Your child's ex-spouse will then have a claim to part ownership of your home. What happens if your child is on title for your house and he or she gets into financial difficulty? Their creditors could put a lien on that property, and you could even find yourself forced out of your home if it has to be sold to satisfy those claims. In addition, if you are ever deemed incompetent and your child has your power of attorney, they may force you out of your house so they can sell it, rent it out, or move in themselves. It's not a pleasant thought, but it is a possibility.

In the end, putting your child on title to your principal residence is just not worth it. Besides, how much are you really saving if you do? The highest provincial probate fee is a mere 1.5 percent in Ontario. So, depending on the province you live in, you might end up saving $700, $800, or even $1,000. That compares to potential tax liabilities for your child in the tens of thousands of dollars, so don't do it.

PART 9

Planned Charitable Giving

In 2004, we started talking about structured giving, planned charitable giving's evolution, after tax rule changes eliminated most "gifts-in-kind" donation strategies. Most investors are already aware that donations to registered charities produce tax credits they can use against 75 percent of their current income. These credits can be carried forward for up to five years and they can be transferred to a spouse at any time to reduce their taxes. In addition, tax credits for charitable giving are 100 percent deductible on a terminal tax return and those credits can be carried back for up to one year before the taxpayer's death.

The most basic form of charitable giving is a pretty cut-and-dried process. You write a cheque to, say, the Canadian Cancer Society for $100, you get a receipt back for the whole amount and are then eligible for tax credits equal to about 40 percent, depending on the top rate in your province. That kind of charitable giving is fine for most investors, but there are other forms of structured giving that are more complex but still very beneficial.

One of these structured giving strategies is known as the "leveraged donation." In this case, you write the charity a cheque for $1,450, they lend you $8,550, and you get a tax receipt back for $10,000. You can then write off the whole $10,000 against your income tax and get a credit of between $4,000 and $5,000—again, depending on your province—but it only costs you $1,450. To discharge the loan, you make a one-time security deposit worth somewhere around $1,450 which is, in turn, deposited in some kind of hedge fund strategy that can pay off the loan in less than 10 years. If the loan is discharged in the agreed-upon time frame, you have no problem; if not, then any amount not discharged will require a proportionate return of tax credits.

This charitable giving strategy works well for several reasons. First, having only invested about $2,900 in cash, you are getting back all of your money in the form of the tax credits and you have a significant cash advantage—basically all your costs, plus maybe 60 percent on top. You also get up to a 10-year tax deferral on that money. That is what is known in the industry as structured giving, and it is a very effective way to reduce your tax burden. And in a terminal return, it is a great way to pay the tax on the estate because it is a deductible against 100 percent of the net income of the estate.

A second concept is the trust structure pioneered by the Canadian Humanitarian Trust. The approach also provides a 60 percent benefit. You make a cash gift to a charitable foundation. Then you apply to a trust to become a Class A beneficiary to receive a grant of pharmaceuticals you gift to a second foundation. You receive one receipt for the cash and a second for the net value of the pharmaceuticals. (Structured donations are discussed in more detail in Section C: A Life Less Taxing.)

Another charitable giving strategy involves the use of the annuity structure. If you were, for example, a 75-year-old retired person, you could put $100,000 into an annuity with a specific charity designated as the beneficiary. First of all, you would receive a tax receipt for the residual value of the annuity, or what it might be worth on the day you die 20 years hence. That could be about 25 percent of the total, or $25,000, and it is that amount that actually goes to the charity upon your demise. Meanwhile, you would also receive the income stream from that annuity for life, which could amount to an annual seven or eight percent tax-free return on your money. So this approach is a beneficial one for the investor and it also helps out the charity, and that's what structured giving is suppose to do.

You could also buy a life insurance policy and make your estate the beneficiary. Then, when you die, you could direct the executor of your estate in your will to give the proceeds of the policy to the charity of your choice. If you were to buy a $100,000 insurance policy today it might cost you $10,000. When you die, your estate will receive $100,000 tax-free, non-probatable dollars which you can then donate posthumously. The charity will get the money, which is a good thing, and your estate will receive a receipt for the full amount, which in turn will entitle your estate to claim tax credits of between $40,000 and $50,000. So by using this charitable giving structure, you will eliminate $40,000 to $50,000 in taxes payable by your estate at the time of your death at a cost of only $10,000.

Gifts-in-kind, or the donation of capital assets to a charity, are still permissible under the current tax rules in some cases. For example, the law permits individuals to donate personal property such as "rare" or "collectible" works of art under the Cultural Properties Review Act. But, to be clear, we are not talking about "Dogs Playing Poker" here; this has to be bona fide, expensive, collectible art.

You can also donate investment real estate properties or environmental lands to a registered charity and get a receipt for that donation based on fair market value. Technically, you can even make a "profitable" gift, but you cannot have acquired the property for the sole purpose of giving it away as a donation and you must have held title on the property for at least three years.

No matter what charitable giving structure you choose, they can all be beneficial depending on your particular circumstances. Unfortunately, charitable giving is a grossly underused tax and financial planning strategy that is a very powerful tool for mitigating tax in the estate and is also very effective on RRSP/RRIF meltdown. But besides the financial benefits to you, charitable giving also helps make the world a better place, which may be the greatest benefit of all.

PART 10

Avoiding Probate Fees

Some people will go to outrageous lengths to avoid paying probate fees, but you should really do your best not to go *too* crazy. If you ask most professionals in the financial planning business, they will tell you it is OK to try to avoid paying too much at probate, but it is not OK to overdo it.

Gifting cash, for example, is generally a good strategy for removing money from your estate in order to limit the impact of probate. But once you start doing things like gifting capital assets, creating deemed dispositions, or trying to put family members on title for assets, you end up creating nothing but headaches. Obviously it's not worth it to go out of your way to save a few thousand in probate fees when you only create, perhaps, tens of thousands in liabilities.

Segregated mutual funds are not probatable assets. Therefore, they often make a good probate-reduction strategy for people over the age of 65 in spite of their higher cost. Likewise, insurance proceeds are generally not probatable assets. Annuities—again, not probatable assets. All of these strategies can make good sense for older investors interested in minimizing the impact of probate on their estate, and are worth looking into.

Regardless of which of these strategies you utilize, in all cases they must have designated beneficiaries, which can be your spouse or another family member, and that then eliminates the question of probate. In the case of assets in an RRSP or a RRIF, if they are transferred to the surviving spouse or a minor child under the age of 18, especially with disability or liability issues, that also eliminates the issue of probate. Similarly, joint accounts held at a bank are also not probatable, and a surviving family member can take over the account without any problem. Your house or principal residence, on the other hand, is a probatable asset. However, it is not subject to capital gains tax as long as it remains in your estate.

Finally, it is also important to remember that financial institutions like to see probated documents, a death certificate, and a will before they release assets belonging to a deceased person. They simply have to; it is the only way for the financial institution to avoid substantial liability for the non-performance of their fiduciary duty toward their client, alive or dead.

So the bottom line is, we can mitigate probate, but we probably can't eliminate all of it. In many cases it is worth paying a few thousand dollars more in probate costs just to speed up the process and avoid red tape. I have seen individuals who have actually gone to the trouble of creating 10 different wills and breaking their assets up so that each will is probated at the lowest level. It's a perfectly legal approach to estate planning, but hardly a prudent one cost-wise. And unless you've got all kinds of time on your hands to spend at your lawyer's office, it just isn't worth the effort in the end in terms of savings.

PART II

Paying the Tax

We have already discussed how useful insurance can be when it comes to paying the huge tax liability your estate may face on your demise. The simplest approach is to use a straight insurance policy or a term insurance contract; both products create a very cost-effective estate planning strategy because you are, in effect, pre-paying the tax.

The universal life insurance approach gives you the huge tax-deferral zone known as the MTAR, which allows you to shelter large amounts of money for a long term and eliminate probate tax on that amount in your estate. Meanwhile, the insurance component pays the tax on everything else.

If you really want to avoid paying any tax at all on your demise, you could just spend all your money while you are alive and die broke. Believe it or not, there are people out there who think this approach to estate planning is perfectly logical: travel, gamble, eat at fancy restaurants, give money away to people on the street, donate money to charity—do whatever it takes to avoid giving it to the government. Someone even wrote a book about this strategy that was actually called *Die Broke*. Now that might not be such a bad strategy if you have no children to leave assets to or if you have a terminal illness and are fairly confident you will die before you can spend all your money. For the vast majority of people, however, insurance is by far the best strategy, especially universal life, which offers enormous advantages in terms of tax, retirement, estate, and investment planning.

There are still many investors out there, however, who refuse to see the advantages to utilizing an insurance strategy. In an investment environment characterized by record-low interest rates, their thinking goes, why would anybody want to put money into a GIC at three percent or some similar low-return vehicle? Well, if the GIC is inside an insurance policy, that means you are getting your three percent return tax-free. As well as that, the insurance company will also give you a rebate of premiums, which amounts to bonus interest on your investments inside the policy. So you could end up getting, perhaps, one-and-a-quarter percent interest above what your bank pays on your GIC, and getting it all on a tax-free basis with tax-free deferral.

In addition, many of the insurance contracts available in the marketplace today will allow you to use various mutual fund products, hedge funds, income trusts, and market index funds, and they create clones of these inside the policy so that they qualify for tax-free status. What more could any investor want?

The lone exception here, under the Income Tax Act, is the segregated mutual fund. Never purchase a segregated fund within an insurance policy, because the moment the fund is inside it is fully taxable. Mutual funds, on the other hand, are not taxable inside a universal life policy.

But there are still a few points to keep in mind here. What some insurance companies will do is create a derivative of a mainstream mutual fund product and then tack their insurance fees on top, so you could end up paying four or five percent MER within your policy. That's why you have to look at the numbers.

In the final analysis, the key element for every investor to keep in mind when considering universal life insurance, or any other financial planning strategy for that matter, is cost. Regardless of the investment strategy you utilize, costs matter—the cost of mutual funds, management expense ratios over two percent, the cost of insurance premiums, the cost of your investments within the insurance policy. It's a critical thing to understand, and one of the basic elements of proper financial planning, along with managing risk, tax, and cash flow.

PART 12

Going Offshore

It's not surprising that many investors today are saying to themselves, "With all the difficulties and complexities that come with investing in Canada, I'll think I'll just concentrate my investments offshore." Well, guess what? Tax changes that came in in 2000 require Canadian taxpayers to report all worldwide income and worldwide assets, particularly assets worth more than $100,000, such as cottages or vacation properties.

Clearly, offshore investments are no longer the "tax haven" they once were. No matter what you have your money invested in outside of this country, every dollar is now reportable back here in Canada, so it's not really worth the considerable risk in the end. And if you fail to report offshore assets or income, that is a criminal offence under the Income Tax Act—so don't do it.

It's another sad fact that many investors who have sunk their money into these offshore tax havens often discover, to their great dismay, that some or all of their cash somehow disappears into the pockets of foreign criminals or even what they thought were professionals or government officials. Literally thousands of Canadians have lost their shirts investing in bogus companies set up in various Caribbean and Central American countries. Don't get sucked in—no matter how good the deal sounds, it is pure hucksterism in almost all cases.

Unless you have absolutely huge assets, the only reason you should ever consider investing offshore is for asset protection for a business—never for your personal money. Besides, with all the tax planning options that are available to you right here at home, there really is no good reason to risk your money in an unreliable market.

U.S. tax law is another factor that many Canadians must take into consideration when doing their financial and tax planning. Remember, if you have an RRSP in Canada but you spend a lot of time in the U.S., perhaps as a snowbird, the "Closer Connection" rule comes into effect if you are resident in the U.S. for an average of 122 days over a three-year period. If that is the case, you must file a report in the States that demonstrates that your principal connection, in terms of your residence and finances, is to Canada.

In addition, if you are a snowbird you also need to be concerned because the U.S. tax people look on Canadian RRSPs and RRIFs as offshore trusts that may be taxable in that country. And if you decide to withdraw the entire contents of your RRSP or RRIF, in effect collapsing the plan, there is an automatic 25 percent withholding tax in Canada. If you do a regular planned withdrawal from your RRSP or RRIF, where you take out less than 10 percent of the total with each withdrawal, then the withholding tax is reduced to 15 percent.

Thirdly, depending on the state you live in when you are in the U.S., you may not be allowed to issue instructions to your financial advisor in Canada. In terms of U.S. federal law, this is permitted, but there are still several states that have not approved the practice within their specific boundaries.

Finally, if you think you can just pull up stakes and leave for another country, taking all your money and assets with you, you can think again. If you decide to leave Canada and no longer want to be considered a citizen of this country for tax purposes (Conrad Black is one such Canadian who comes to mind here), the law says the act of leaving is consistent with the act of dying. Therefore, it is equivalent to the disposition of all your capital assets. And even though you may not be selling off anything and fully intend to keep some of your assets here in Canada, you still must post a bond in cash or government securities equivalent to the tax liability that was generated by your departure.

So, while investing or moving offshore may not be the tax boon it is often trumped up to be, staying in this country is not as bad as it is often made out to be either. There are, in fact, many effective strategies at your disposal that will allow you to live and invest in Canada and pay minimal tax on your estate. All you have to do is utilize them.

PART 13

Revealing Your Financial Estate Plan

Suddenly your estate plan is no longer just about death, dying, taxes and wills; now it's a *life* plan. The modern investor should think in terms of "life planning" rather than "death planning." You should have a plan in place to manage your finances during the last 30 years of your life that will make them the best 30 years of your life.

During those last 30 years you will want to have enough cash flow, life insurance protection, and security of capital to ensure you are going to be able to do the things you want to do. In short, you are going to want peace of mind, and that's just what proper financial and estate planning will give you.

If the last 30 years of your life are still a way off in the future, you can probably count on a few things being quite different for you during that period of life than they were for your parents. You can expect to live longer, be healthier, and be more physically active. You will probably want to travel, take courses, or maybe go back to school. And there is no reason why you can't do all those things during the last 30 years, but you have to plan accordingly. That means putting plans in place now for cash flow management, tax reduction, cost reduction, and estate management.

The new life plan is a dynamic tool. It evolves as the investment environment changes and as tax rules change from year to year and as the economy rolls up and down. Likewise, your will should be a dynamic tool, as should your tax plan. In essence, your entire financial and estate plan should be dynamic, capable of handling any variation that life may throw at you. No one expects to go through life completely without change—changing jobs, changing homes, even changing spouses—so your financial and estate plan should reflect that reality. But you can take control of the last 30 years of your life simply by taking control of the four key elements of proper financial planning we have talked about: cash, cost, risk, and tax—the X-Factors. If you do it right, the last 30 years of your life will be exactly what they should be: the cream in your coffee and the icing on the cake.

PART 14

The New Estate Imperative

The goal of the New Estate Imperative is simple: to pay minimal tax on your investments, and be as tax-free as possible while remaining tax-compliant and mitigating risk. You want to "risk manage" your assets, protecting yourself from capital loss and, in turn, protecting your lifestyle. You want to ensure that any major potential medical, financial, or tax threat has been planned for. And finally, you want to make sure you have the level of cash flow you will need in retirement to allow you to do the things you want to do.

We want to structure our affairs for maximum tax benefit. We need to recognize the evolutionary changes that have taken place in our economy: interest rates are at record lows; inflation is dead; the Canadian dollar is way up; we are facing potential increases in both provincial and municipal taxes; real estate is booming; and equity markets are volatile at best. There are plenty of opportunities to make money in the current investment environment, but there are also plenty of opportunities to lose it, so the protection of capital at all costs should always be our primary consideration.

We also know today that RRSPs and RRIFs are not the be-all and end-all when it comes to financial planning. We know that structured and planned giving offer excellent tax reduction opportunities. We know that there are legal structures that can give us greater control over our investments and better protect our money. We know that insurance can be a financial and estate planning strategy, not just another cost; it is an investment rather than an expenditure.

If you understand the New Estate Imperative, you can dramatically reduce the taxes you will pay for the rest of your life. Not only that, but you can bullet-proof your estate, bullet-proof your lifestyle, and take control of the rest of your life.

SECTION C

A Life Less Taxing

INTRODUCTION

The Changing Tax Landscape

Why is it so essential to do proper tax planning? The basic reason is that taxes play a huge role in our financial lives. Reports from the Fraser Institute show that in 2003 Canadians, on average, spent 47 percent of their total income in federal, provincial, and municipal taxes. This varies by province, but in some provinces this number was actually closer to 50 percent.

Another reason we need to do proper tax planning is because we are now living in a whole new tax environment today, where things are radically different than they were just a few years ago. For one thing, municipal taxes are going up because real property assessment, or market value assessment, is now recognizing that many properties across Canada have gone up anywhere from five to twenty percent over the last year. In addition, many municipalities are also increasing their mill rates to cover higher expenses due to cuts in provincial and federal funding.

Property taxes are largely uncontrollable for the average taxpayer. Yes, you can appeal the assessments, but other than that, not much else can be done. You should be concerned about the other taxes you pay, however, because many provinces have begun directly or surreptitiously increasing taxes, fees, and other costs as well. You should keep in mind that many of your provincial taxes, especially the provincial income tax, are a percentage of the federal tax. Therefore, if you can reduce your federal tax, you are cutting your provincial taxes at the same time.

The fact is, it is simply impossible to do any kind of investing or retirement planning today without taking into consideration the brave new tax world we are living in. For years people simply maxed out their RRSP contribution and left it at that, but you can't do that anymore. The C.D. Howe Institute has released several reports over the last couple of years that show how RRSPs and RRIFs can actually represent a tax trap for investors, doing little more than building up a substantial tax liability for the average individual in the long term. For lower income people with less than $100,000 invested in their RRSP or RRIF, this tax liability is extraordinarily punitive, and many people are well advised to melt down their RRSPs or RRIFs before the age of 65 to avoid all the punitive claw-backs that they could be hit with.

Believe it or not, having no money in an RRSP in retirement and little or no other investment income would result in you receiving actual benefits from government statutory programs equivalent to $250,000 in RRSPs. Now that doesn't mean you should be spendthrift and not save or invest for retirement, but it does mean you should look at the tax consequences of each investment decision you make. It means you should familiarize yourself with the rule changes that have taken place over the last few years, especially since 1997, such as the four narrow tax brackets, the fact that so many equities are inside RRSPs and RRIFs, and, of course, the fact that you must not only absorb all of your capital losses within your RRSP or RRIF, but when you take the money out it is treated as ordinary income and not as capital gains.

So what's new in terms of tax rules? Plenty. On February 27, 2004, the government introduced 200 pages of new tax law that essentially gave us the final legislation on changes proposed from 2002 onward—and there were also 223 pages of interpretation bulletins to go with that. In addition, the 400-page 2004 budget also made significant changes to the tax code.

At this writing, the government is seriously looking at the elimination of the interest expense deduction for investing. We've seen draft legislation already and consultations continue on this issue. However, primarily because the federal government lost a number of federal court cases and Supreme Court cases on reasonable expectation of profit, you can expect that interest expense incurred for the generation of capital gains eventually will be eliminated altogether, unless it can be applied against other income, specifically interest or dividends. The idea that you're borrowing money to generate capital gains just won't cut it anymore.

As if higher taxes weren't enough, these changes to the tax rules come at a time when we are experiencing a real decline in investment income. In 2003, personal investment income, despite a rising stock market, declined by about 12.5 percent. Therefore, individual investors, in many cases, are no longer making good returns on their money but they are paying more in taxes. In addition, another C.D. Howe Institute report has shown that Canadian business capital taxes are 11.4 percent higher than those in the United States, causing significant capital outflows in this economy.

All of these factors demonstrate why every investor needs to change the way they look at tax planning now. Your objective is to be in control of the taxes you pay, and you do that, first, by knowing the rules. Those who don't may soon find that their life has become substantially more taxing.

i. Take a current economic snapshot

All financial planning should be done in the context of the current economic reality. In the early part of 2004, for example, we saw a negative gross domestic product in Canada. This was primarily due to the fact that the U.S. economy was soaring because the U.S. government cut taxes. That tax relief was comprehensive, affecting dividends, capital gains, and overall income, as well as estate taxes.

Therefore, with the Canadian economy stalled and the Canadian dollar rising rapidly in value relative to the U.S.

dollar, it became essential for Canadian investors to be especially careful in the way they managed their money. In addition, inflation is currently running at about 2.1 percent and GIC rates are now at 40-year lows of about 3.75 percent for five years. When you take out tax and inflation, needless to say, a 0.3 percent return for most people just won't cut it. That's $300 on a $100,000 GIC.

Security has also become a major issue in the current economic environment, both personal and financial. The unemployment rate remains around 7.6 percent and could rise. We are losing many jobs through outsourcing, especially in manufacturing, due to both the high operating costs in North America and the high Canadian dollar. In addition, fears about terrorism have added to security costs, especially at airports and border crossings, resulting in essentially a new tax on all of us.

With all of these things to consider, our current economic snapshot is clearly not an inviting one for most investors—but there's more. Only after you throw in factors like U.S. tariffs against Canadian products such as softwood lumber and wheat, and concerns about BSE, or mad cow disease, can you begin to get a true idea of the current economic context of our times. Also, high energy and oil prices are likely here to stay. And when you combine all that with higher provincial and municipal taxes and equity markets in real uncertainty, things are not likely to get much better for investors for quite some time. Still, that is the unique economic context we all have to deal with today; and the sooner you learn to do that, that better. Things have clearly changed dramatically since the 1990s, and that means it's going to take new ideas and new strategies to put you in control of the taxes you pay.

ii. Tax reporting versus tax planning

Contrary to popular belief, tax planning is a year-round activity. Unfortunately, most Canadians believe that tax planning simply means going to a tax preparation service in the latter part of April to do a tax filing for the prior year. But that is, in fact, tax *reporting,* and we can't do anything after January 1 of the following year until we do take care of that—unless, of course, it is the proverbial RRSP contribution, which, as we have said, only creates tax liability down the road. Tax *planning,* however, should be done long before December 31. At least it should be if you want to be in control of the taxes you pay.

Why are we doing tax planning? Well first of all, to control our overall cash flow. If we can maximize our available credits and deductions early in the year, we can then move to reduce our instalments and eliminate withholding taxes. This, in turn, may significantly improve cash flow and better shelter our investment returns so that our money grows on a tax-deferred or tax-free basis. Obviously, if you can have compounded tax-reduced, tax-deferred, or tax-free returns, you're going to make an awful lot more money.

Tax planning is especially important for people over the age of 65 in the current tax context because of the many new taxes targeted specifically at retirement income. For example, if you are over 65 and your income exceeds, $27,000 a year, you are in danger of losing your age tax credit or, more accurately, the government clawing it back. In addition, if your aggregate income, which includes the gross up of dividends plus capital gains but not minus losses, exceeds about $59,000 a year, you will lose most, if not all, of your Old Age Security over time. The government will simply claw that back with a 15 percent clawback tax.

In addition, we are only starting to understand the severity of the situation with regard to the four narrow tax brackets recently introduced by the government. These brackets are so close together that if your income starts to move beyond $35,000 and you are over 65, every additional incremental dollar you receive, such as from an RRIF withdrawal, means you can be hit with progressively higher taxes.

Keeping these factors in mind, we have to think and prepare accordingly. Proper tax planning can give you more control over the taxes you pay, and better tax planning inevitably leads to better cash flow and better accumulation of wealth in the long term. In order to make life a lot less taxing, we have to look at four basic components:

1. how we earn our income,

2. income splitting,

3. maximizing deferrals, and

4. maximizing deductions.

PART I

How We Earn Our Income

i. Capital gains and dividends

How we earn our income is critical; this is, of course, part one of proper tax planning. Capital gains, for example, are both an excellent source of retirement income and an excellent tax planning strategy because they are taxed at a reduced rate, with only 50 percent being included for tax purposes. This applies to any Canadian-controlled, private corporation that is in business for two or more years, does not trade in real estate, and has 50 percent or more of their assets domiciled in Canada.

Remember, too, that you still have the $500,000 capital gains exemption when you sell your business. This would also include a family farm, as long as it's incorporated. Similarly, dividends are exposed to a dividend tax credit if they come from a Canadian company. Once again, this reduces the effective tax rate on dividends from a Canadian source.

It is important to keep in mind, however, that interest income is taxed at the same high rate as ordinary income. Therefore, unless the interest income is at a very high level, it is hardly attractive today. If you can get an asset-backed security or a mortgage-backed security paying between eight and ten percent, interest income might be worthwhile. But since most fixed income products produce almost no return after tax and inflation, this is usually not an effective strategy.

ii. Bonds

As for Canada Savings Bonds as a source of retirement income, they are just not worth it from a tax perspective. Outside a registered investment, you don't get any cash flow for five years, but you still have to report the accrued interest on your tax form and pay income tax for five years on money you don't get.

iii. Annuities

Certain types of annuities can be attractive retirement income options. While standard annuities may not appear attractive in the current environment because of low interest rates, a product called a "prescribed annuity" is an exception. A prescribed annuity is one that is prescribed as to cash flow, meaning it guarantees what the cash flow is going to be for the life of the annuity. As a result, you know exactly what you're going to get. And since annuity cash flow is largely considered a remission of capital, you don't really have to worry about paying much tax. If you're over 65 and receiving income from an annuity, it is treated the same as pension income and you qualify for the $1,000 pension income tax credit, so it makes it a tad attractive for many individuals.

iv. Structured withdrawal

Strategies such as systematic withdrawal plans from open account mutual fund products also offer an effective retirement income strategy. If you have mutual funds outside an RRSP, properly structured, you should be able to make a capital withdrawal of about eight percent a year for the first six years and have no taxable income since it will be considered a return of your original investment capital. Thereafter, it's more of a blended payment with some degree of taxation, mostly capital gains.

v. Universal life insurance

Many Canadian taxpayers, especially higher-net-worth people, are now gravitating toward universal life insurance. Why? Well, if you have money inside an investment account inside an insurance policy, the Income Tax Act allows you to create an insured pension plan. This creates a tax-free cash flow, since any of the money you get from the plan is considered simply a loan borrowed against the plan's capital, and therefore not taxable income. This has become a very important strategy and an especially attractive one for individuals who want to avoid all the clawback taxes and seniors' taxes. A universal life policy is also an excellent destination for the proceeds from the sale of a business practice, farm, investment real estate, or RRSP/RRIF meltdown.

vi. Trusts

Income trusts have been around for quite some time, but more and more Canadians have been utilizing this strategy in recent years. In fact, today we have over $90-billion domiciled inside income trusts. Again, part of the cash flow you get from a trust is considered a return of capital, so there is some tax amelioration in owning such an investment.

vii. Real estate (principal residence)

Another source of retirement income, believe it or not, is your principal residence. Your principal residence is tax-free, although many Canadians are of the mistaken belief that their house will be exposed to tax when they die. The provinces do charge an estate administration tax—a probate fee—ranging from a low of $75 in some provinces to a high of 1.5 percent of the value of the property, but other than that, there are no other taxes on the principal residence, not when you die and not when you sell one. That is, of course, as long as you don't sell a principal residence more than once a year and you don't own more than two pieces of residential or investment property. Basically, you are allowed one principal residence per family at any given time, and you could actually buy and sell one every 12 months and have a tax-free capital gain.

viii. RESPs

Registered educational savings plans, or RESPs, can offer another good retirement income strategy because the money earned inside these plans grows on a tax-deferred basis for up to 25 years. Also, when you put money into an RESP on behalf of a minor 17 and under, it qualifies for the Canadian Educational Savings Grant which is a tax-free grant of up 20 percent of what you put in up to $400 a year on a $2,000 contribution. If the family's income is below $35,000, that contribution grant is bumped up by an additional $100, and if the family's income is between $35,000 and $70,000 there's an additional $50, making for a maximum of $500 or $450 per year depending on your income and contribution.

Unbeknownst to most people, since 1998 every Canadian taxpayer can be the beneficiary of an RESP. You don't get the federal grant if you are over 17, but you do still qualify for the up to 25 years of tax deferral. To get the money out of the RESP, all you have to do is register for an educational program of 13 weeks' duration or greater, and that's a small price to pay for such a great tax deferral benefit. Plus, your capital in the plan, which can be up to $42,000, can be extracted on a tax-free basis, unlike capital in an RRSP/RRIF, which is, of course, taxed as ordinary income.

PART 2

Income Splitting

Income splitting was devised a great many years ago and remains one of the most attractive tax-reduction strategies available. The theory behind income splitting is straightforward enough: if one spouse is earning substantial income and the other one is earning nothing, it might be attractive to put income into the hands of the low-income partner, thus allowing them to pay a minimal tax on that income and reducing the overall tax burden for the entire family.

So the basic idea behind income splitting is to put money in the hands of other potential taxpayers in the same family, but that "splitting" of income can only happen within strict limitations. If, for example, you simply try to give some of your income to your spouse, that money will be taxed back in your name; you can't just gift somebody your income. Likewise, if they borrow the money and you guarantee the loan, once again, there will be attribution of that income back to you. However, if that person borrows the money and you pay the interest on the loan only, there can be no attribution.

You can, in fact, make a loan to that family member, not a gift but a loan, but it must be an interest-bearing demand loan and you must have a loan certificate. There must be an agreement between the two parties involved and you must collect the interest on that loan at the prescribed rate by January 31 of the subsequent year and report it on your income tax. That is the only way the income earned by the family member will be taxed in their hands. Therefore, according to the rules of attribution, if you were to lend your spouse money and the prescribed interest rate is four percent and they are able to make eight after investing that money, four percent of that income will end up in their hands on a net basis.

The same thing applies with minor children. If you gift money to a child, grandchild, niece, nephew, or adopted child who is under the age of 18, and that money is invested to earn interest or dividends, there is what's called an attribution. The income is taxed in your hands, not their hands, and the net result is higher taxes for you. Another option, however, is to set up what is called a bare trust, which involves filling out and filing a one-page trust document you can get from any financial planner; the whole process takes about three weeks. In the case of a bare trust, you are allowed to place money in the trust as a donor while some other family member acts essentially as the trustee. The money in the trust can then be invested where it can earn more than $16,000 a year in tax-free capital gains on behalf of the child, or the beneficiary, inside the plan. This is a very effective strategy for achieving proper income splitting.

If you have an incorporated business, it is often a good strategy to pay compensation to your family members so that all the income of the business is not attributed to you, resulting, of course, in a potentially very high personal income tax rate. However, in order to successfully split the compensation among family members, each case must first pass the "reasonableness" test. That means that the compensation being paid by your business to your family member must be reasonable compared to what you would normally pay for a third-party individual hired in the open market. In addition, if your spouse is a shareholder of your company and has no other income, is not being paid a salary, and the business is profitable, you can pay out dividends equivalent to about $30,000 to that spouse on a tax-free basis because of the dividend tax credits.

It is important to understand how to do proper income splitting with regard to other factors such as Canada Pension. As long as your spouse is over 60, if you are collecting CPP you can split up to half of CPP income into your spouse's hands up to a maximum of about $4,000 a year. That is an important factor, because if your spouse has little or no income and you have substantial income plus an RRIF withdrawal, you can reduce your taxes and maybe save as much as $2,000 a year by doing that type of income split.

Clearly, income splitting can be a very effective strategy when it comes to tax planning. But how you earn your income involves planning as well, taking into account elements like the amelioration of capital gains and dividends and other types of income structures and the use of tax-deferred vehicles or tax-reduced vehicles. It does take some effort to learn about your options, but the final pay-off is more than worth the effort.

PART 3
Maximizing Deferrals

The basic idea behind tax deferral is this: you put off paying a portion of your taxes now so that you can pay them later in life, ostensibly because your income will likely go down after you retire and you will, therefore, end up paying less tax in the future.

There are currently a number of tax deferral strategies available for investors. You can, for example, accumulate profits in your business and not pay out the dividends and/or salary. You can utilize tax deferment structures such as RRSPs or RRIFs, although you have to understand that these vehicles represent a long-term tax liability. And you can, of course, look at other types of tax structures such as universal life insurance.

Universal life allows you to buy insurance to pay the taxes on your estate on your

> "Investors need to recall that the return *of* capital is more important than the return *on* capital. "
> —*Stanley Taube, attorney, writing in the* Globe & Mail.

demise while at the same time creating a tax-free zone called the MTAR, or maximum taxable actuarial reserve. Therefore, if you put money inside the investment account in your insurance policy, it can grow on a tax-deferred basis literally for the rest of your life, and whatever is inside the investment account on your demise will come out tax- and probate-free. In some provinces, there is a premium tax of two to three percent on the earnings, but other than that there are no other taxes to be paid. In addition, the insurance company will let you borrow against your investment account and that borrowing, with the capitalization of interest, is considered a non-taxable income stream.

Now, there is of course the question of proper planning

with respect to real estate because, again, you don't pay capital gains tax on accumulation. You only pay capital gains tax when you sell something and realize, or crystallize, the gain. Therefore, with capital assets we are allowed long-term tax deferral as a result. So tax deferral today, while substantially reduced because of the progressive liability of RRSPs and RRIFs, is still a possibility with proper planning.

PART 4

Maximizing Deductions

The final element of creating a life less taxing is maximizing every tax deduction and tax credit available to you. Although only a limited number remain as of this writing, when properly utilized, these deductions and credits offer fantastic tax planning opportunities. Because laws can change from year to year, remember to check with a financial professional before implementing any of these strategies

i. Flow-through shares

Flow-through shares are an excellent tax-deferral vehicle that has been around since about 1988. Flow-through shares take advantage of a specific tax law with respect to Canadian oil, gas, and mining companies. When these kinds of companies do exploration and development, the Income Tax Act permits them to write off 100 percent of their development and exploration costs. However, if the oil, gas, or mining company does not need to write off these costs, they can be sold to a general partner who assembles a portfolio of write-offs from various public and private oil, gas, and mining companies, along with some of their various public or private stock.

You might pay $2,500 for a share in this type of portfolio—it may consist of the write-offs of 10, 15, or 20 different public and private oil, gas, and mining companies as well as a portfolio of their stocks—and that portfolio becomes, essentially, like a tax-deductible mutual fund investment for you. But your $2,500 investment may result in $2,500 in various tax deductions that are deductible against your total income. Then, a year-and-a-half to two years later, shares in the portfolio become liquid and can be converted into the individual stocks or to a mutual fund.

When you sell that collection of stocks, of course, you

may have a crystallized capital gain. But because you've got a 100 percent write-off to begin with, the adjusted cost base—your cost of those stocks or funds—is considered to be zero. Therefore, what you've done is taken ordinary income, from an RRSP/RRIF withdrawal, salaried income, or other income being taxed at the highest rates, and essentially deferred it for 18 months to two years down the road where it is taxed at a much lower rate, the capital gains rate, which is half the regular rate.

Of course, you don't *have* to sell those stocks or mutual funds two years down the road. You can hold on to them for as long as you want, and when you finally do decide to sell them, that is when you will pay the tax. You can gift the shares to a registered charity for a fair market value tax credit or roll them over every two years for additional deductions.

ii. Leveraged limited partnerships

Another tax deduction strategy that may work for you is called the "leveraged limited partnership" or "leveraged limited tax partnership." Like flow-through shares, the leveraged limited tax partnerships are deductible against your total income, reducing what's called your net taxable income and increasing your personal deductions. (Interest expense reduction, or deduction as we've looked at it, may not be available by the time you read this, but if it remains in place you would be well advised to take full advantage of it even though there are record-low interest rates.)

What exactly is a leveraged limited tax partnership? All companies, public as well as private, incur substantial "soft" costs. These include things such as advertising, salary, rent, and other related expenses that could accumulate to millions of dollars and often create losses for the company. In order to mitigate these costs, the company can set up a limited partnership. You can then give money to the company through the limited partnership to help pay the company's bills and in return you get substantial write-offs without putting up 100 percent of the money needed. Therefore, you are not actually getting a $100 write-off for a $100 investment; you are getting a $100 write-off for perhaps a $30 cost, and the rest is called "leverage."

So, for example, let's say you want to reduce your total taxable income by $10,000 because you took an additional $10,000 from your RRIF as a meltdown strategy. You could accomplish this by buying $10,000 worth of a leveraged limited tax partnership. First, you would write a cheque for $3,000 to the company and the company would then arrange for you to be lent, without a credit application or approval, $7,000 that would not appear on your credit record. You would then be allowed to write off $10,000 against your income. By any measure, that's an effective tax deduction strategy.

To pay off the loan, the company will devote a substantial portion of its total sales over the next few years to assist you in paying off that $7,000 loan. Alternatively, at various times, usually at each year end, the company will let you convert some of that limited partnership back into the publicly traded stock of that company. Then, after selling a portion of that stock to discharge the loan, you will still end up with substantial stock in your hands at no cost. You have, therefore, effectively reduced your taxes by $10,000 and ended up with a block of stock at no cost to you, allowing you to make a substantial capital gain. What makes the leveraged limited partnership such an effective tax deduction strategy is the fact you are writing off real costs incurred by the company, public or private. This means there is a clear audit trail here—and sometimes two audits, in light of recent scandals and concerns.

When limited partnerships are combined with other tax deduction strategies such as flow-through shares, the interest expense deduction, and other personal deductions, we are able to better reduce our total taxable income down to what's called our net taxable income. Unfortunately, in Canada we have an item of legislation called the alternative minimum tax that places a limit on how low we can go with our net taxable income. The purpose of the alternative minimum tax is to say no matter who you are, you have to pay tax on something; at this writing you can only tax-plan down to $40,000. Therefore, using all the tax reduction strategies at our disposal, plus RRSP contributions and other items, we can reduce our net taxable income, or our NTI, down to $40,000 for the purpose of alternative minimum tax.

iii. Other strategies for the tax year

Just because you have tax-planned down to the alternative minimum doesn't mean you're finished. You could further shelter the remaining $40,000, or a substantial portion of that, by taking a charitable tax deduction against 75 percent of the net taxable income through the use of various innovative structures such as a leveraged donation plan or a structured donation tax credit.

It is important to remember that tax credits are as good as cash, and worth twice the value of deductions. They are, in fact, the prepayment of taxes, rather than deductions. The law permits you to use tax credits against 75 percent of your net taxable income, even with the alternative minimum tax, in order to reduce your total taxes by 75 percent. That goes to 100 percent when a terminal tax return is filed in the year you die. Plus, tax credits can be carried back to one year before you die and applied against taxes already paid.

Meanwhile, deductions or credits, specifically discretionary credits like charitable donation credits, can be transferred to a spouse and have a five-year carry-forward. Could you get anything more powerful and more flexible for the taxpayer? Tax credits are a little-known and under-utilized strategy, but they represent an enormous tax planning opportunity.

While the gifts-in-kind plan may still benefit rich people, for the average middle-income taxpayer it is no longer a possibility. But all taxpayers can still benefit from leveraged donation tax credits and structured giving plans, and these are strategies you should take full advantage of if at all possible.

All kinds of taxpayers can take advantage of deduction strategies: if you are selling a business, a practice, or a farm; if you are selling a milk quota, egg quota, or chicken quota because you are a farmer; if you are properly melting down, not collapsing, an RRSP or RRIF by taking out $5,000 at a time to reduce the withholding taxes; if you have investment real estate that you are selling; or if you have received a termination allowance at the completion of a work program. Each of these situations can be effectively planned and taxes reduced if you maximize the deductions and tax credits available. It's simple: deductions allow us to dramatically reduce our overall tax bill, and that leads to reduced instalments and reduced withholding taxes at source. If you utilize all available deductions and credits, you can file a tax form called a T12/13 for salaried individuals to reduce your withholding tax on your salary and regular compensation.

The net result of all of this tax planning is improved cash flow for you, and you can then take that improved cash flow and do something with it. It's called a "redeployment"—you take the liberated cash and redeploy it in liberated tax zones, or "locations" as we now call them. Liberated cash must not be put back into a maximum tax environment; the whole purpose of tax planning is to shelter your cash flow and then to put it into an environment that is tax-reduced, tax-deferred, or even tax-free, such as universal life insurance. Once inside the location, you can then move on to the allocation phase, planning how you are going to divvy the cash up among equities, bonds, currency, and so on. But you can't do that until you have liberated your cash from those high-tax environments.

For example, if you had $100,000 in additional cash from something like an RRSP/RRIF meltdown or the sale of a farm or investment real estate, that $100,000 would be exposed to tax at the highest rate as part of your total income. However, by using various types of flow-through share or limited partnership strategies you could reduce your taxes dramatically. You could buy $60,000 of a tax-advantaged limited partnership at a cost of $18,000 and reduce your net taxable income to $40,000. You could then use a structured (trust) or leveraged tax plan through charitable giving to shelter a further $30,000 of that $40,000 net taxable income. The net result would be only $10,000 exposed to tax, so instead of paying tax on $100,000, you would pay tax on only $10,000. That is an obviously substantial savings of 90 percent on your tax bill. And the best thing about this strategy is that it is completely compliant with tax rules, meaning no problems with Canada Customs and Revenue down the road. Once again, proper planning is everything.

Charitable tax credits are issued at the top rate of your province of domicile. So if, for example, you live in Saskatchewan, the rate is 44.5 percent, or $4,450 in tax credits on a $10,000 donation. In Ontario, it would be $4,640; in British Columbia, approximately $4,370; and in Alberta, about $3,900.

v. Structured donation plans

Structured donation plans and structured giving are relatively new tax planning strategies that also offer excellent tax reduction benefits that are totally compliant with all existing tax laws. In fact, in both cases, whether you are talking about leveraged donations or structured (trust) donation plans, major national law firms have prepared excruciatingly detailed written legal tax opinions regarding these strategies in light of the December 5, 2003, tax rule changes, the legislative changes established on February 27, 2004, and all the budget documents.

In order to explain how a structured donation plan strategy works, we can examine one plan called the Canadian Humanitarian Trust (CHT). The CHT was established to provide support for recognized Canadian charitable organizations that assist in the relief of suffering around the world. One of the CHT's main activities is sourcing pharmaceuticals and medical supplies on the World Health Organization supplier list that are used for the treatment of AIDS and HIV as well as intestinal parasites. These supplies are then dispensed through major aid organizations, such as Feed the Children, which act as distributors in Africa, South America, Asia, and the Middle East.

Any individual or corporation can make a formal application to the CHT to become a beneficiary, and acceptance is based in part upon the past history and/or current intent of the applicant to provide financial support for qualified Canadian charities whose mandate includes offering humanitarian relief. Individual and corporate applicants who qualify as beneficiaries are, in turn, encouraged to donate their trust property, pharmaceutical units in this case, to worthy Canadian registered charities.

The charitable foundation will receive the units and distribute them as gifts to various charities and the donor, you, will receive two receipts. One receipt is for 100 percent of the cash donation that you made. The second receipt is for the net value of the pharmaceutical units, and the tax credits will be based on independent valuations of those units by noted national and international experts. Because the cash portion of the donation for the tax credit is substantial, what you are going to end up with is a tax credit that is far greater than your cash cost. Usually, depending on your province of jurisdiction, the tax credit is worth in excess of 40 percent of the adjusted cost base of the total units. (In Ontario, for example, the credit would be 46.41 percent of the appraised value.) That will go up or down depending on your province of residence, but it is still a very substantial tax credit in any case.

So let's say, for example, that you decide to purchase units in a structured donation plan valued at $100,000. If you wish to get a tax receipt for the full $100,000, it will cost you about $30,500 in cash up front; that is the cash donation component. But the pharmaceutical units themselves will also have an adjusted cost base of $69,500, bringing the total amount to $100,000. If you are an Ontario resident, you will get tax credits equivalent to 46.41 percent of the total, or $46,410. Therefore, your cash advantage, because you paid $30,500 in cash up front, is $15,910. In other words, you are getting back all your initial cash along with a net cash benefit of over 50 percent.

You could borrow the money to make that initial cash donation, but the interest would not be deductible. In spite of that, considering the short-term cost and the record-low interest rates, you are still going to be in an overwhelmingly cash positive position. Remember, this deduction amount and the tax credits yielded will be deductible against 75 percent of your net taxable income.

As an additional benefit, there is no capital gains tax payable on this type of donation. As the beneficiary of a trust, you are deemed to have acquired the pharmaceutical units at the same cost basis as the trust itself. Current Canadian tax law states that the adjusted cost base is equal to the fair market value of the unit. And because the independent appraisers have determined the fair market value, there is, therefore, no capital gains tax or other taxes to be paid by the donor. (According to Canada Customs and Revenue, fair market value generally means the highest price that a property would bring expressed in dollars in an open and unrestricted market between a willing buyer and a seller who are knowledgeable, informed, and prudent, and who are acting independently of each other. Fair market value does not include any amounts paid or payable to other parties such as commissions to sales agents or sales taxes like the goods and services tax or harmonized sales tax or provincial sales tax.)

But, you may ask, how do you report all of this on your tax return? As an approved donor, you will receive a package that includes all of the required documentation as well as a step-by-step checklist outlining how to report this transaction on your personal tax return. Once again, this process is called structured giving, and if it sounds a bit complicated, don't worry, it really isn't.

Whether you use leveraged donation, structured giving (trust), or both, the objective is to generate maximum tax credits to reduce your total taxes payable. The various deductions you create, along with your personal deductions, interest expense, limited partnerships, and various types of flow-through shares, combine to reduce your total income down to the net taxable amount. You can then use these tax credit strategies to shelter 75 percent of your net taxable income.

The potential tax reduction you can realize by utilizing these strategies is substantial, and they can put you on the road to making your life a lot less taxing, now and in the future.

Conclusion

So where do you go from here? Remember the four key tax planning components we have discussed: knowing your sources of income; income splitting; maximizing deferrals; and maximizing deductions. The goal is to liberate as much of your money as possible from taxing environments. Once your money is liberated from taxation, you can then begin to place it in the right locations, locations that are tax-deferred, tax-reduced, or even tax-free. These are known as the tax freedom zones in the Income Tax Act. When your money is properly located, you can start to make more tax-effective returns, using various structured investment strategies such as universal life insurance or back-to-back annuities.

But it is important to act now. These tax structures and tax planning options may not last, and the earlier in the tax year you act, the better your overall cash flow will be. Remember, the less you pay in taxes now, the more you will be able to invest to make even better returns down the road. How do you make your life less taxing? You do it by taking control of your finances through proper planning today.

SECTION D
Back-to-Basics Investing

PART I

Back-to-Basics Investing

If you want to understand the basic principles that lie at the core of personal financial planning and investment strategy, you really need to go back to the 1930s. That's when Benjamin Graham and David Dodd were developing the whole process of stock analysis and how to determine stock value. These men first put forth their ideas in 1934 in the book *Security Analysis,* and their concept of value investing has been influencing our lives ever since. The sequel to that book, *The Intelligent Investor*, published in 1949, has become a core text in the field.

The 1930s and '40s do seem like a long time ago in terms of our financial world, but the basic theories regarding investing put forward at that time are still relevant today. For example, if Professor Graham was rewriting *The Intelligent Investor* now, revised and updated for our contemporary times, we would likely find that he would still recommend investing in large companies rather than small ones. He also believed that investors should look to buy companies that have assets at least twice as great as their current liabilities and that long-term debt should not exceed working capital. This is still sound advice today.

In addition, Graham also argued that any company an investor is considering should not have reported losses any time in the last 10 years. Prospective companies should also have a strong history of paying dividends wherever possible, and the current stock price should not be more than 15 times its average earnings for the past three years. Considered together, these points of analysis play an essential role in giving the investor some idea of the intrinsic value of a given stock. This method of analysis, created decades ago, still lies at the heart of proper financial planning and investment strategy today.

Another landmark text in the field of financial planning

and investment strategy was *Common Stocks and Uncommon Profits,* published in 1958 by Phil Fisher. Mr. Fisher, who died in 2004, was another value investor who tried to find those undervalued gems, the large companies in the marketplace that are trading at unique values. Like Graham, Fisher's approach to investing is as valid today as it was when he published his book, although it seems to come in and out of fashion from time to time.

For example, in a recent article, James Cramer, editor and founder of thestreet.com and one of the great gurus of the high-tech stock boom, pointed out very clearly that blue-chips offer enormous value for most investors. In his regular column in *New York Magazine*, Mr. Cramer went on to say that when you can find great value companies among the super blue-chips, the biggest and the best trading at dirt cheap prices, clearly this is the time to buy. He even mentioned some of the stocks we've talked about as great undervalued investments—Exxon, General Electric, Microsoft, and AIG. Ironically, he also warned very strongly against investing in companies such as Tyco, Lucent, Nortel, and Time-Warner, all stocks he used to recommend back in 1999 when everyone was jumping on the "new economy" bandwagon.

Princeton economist Burton Malkiel also focuses on core investment philosophies in his book *A Random Walk Down Wall Street,* especially with regard to index investing. Malkiel obviously likes Graham's focus on cheap stocks, and he likes the idea of looking for value, but he argues that underpriced stocks are very hard to find and therefore it is impossible to outperform most indexes over time. Still, Malkiel continues to recommend buying stocks with above average earnings growth over the last five years if at all possible and stocks that have firm foundations in value—in other words, cheap stocks that could grow.

Yet, although he talks a lot about stocks, Malkiel is basically an indexer. He suggests putting money into equities, but also buying the index wherever possible because he feels that there would be regression back to the mean and that most portfolio managers could not outperform markets over time. He does cite all sorts of exceptions, but these are really aberrations that don't last over the long term.

But again, when you buy an index, what are you really getting? You are getting the valuation of the total market. But when two or three stocks dominate an index, as has often been the case, you are trapped in the same basic problem: you end up buying that overvalued company anyway. So indexes do have a role, but we have to tread carefully.

A study of index investing published in 2004 suggested that wherever you buy the index, the product offering the lowest fees is probably the best strategy. This would include products such as an exchange traded fund that also segments many indexes into specialty collections and can be actively traded, mainly because the fees are probably dramatically less. If, for example, your bank is offering you an index mutual fund at 150 basis points and you can buy an exchange traded fund for, perhaps, 35 basis points, needless to say, the cheaper one will perform better over time. The same study went on to look at the whole question of active trading and it pointed out that, unfortunately, some of the funds with the highest fees did, in fact, outperform over time, earning back not only their outrageous fees but also significant returns above and beyond the market. However, these funds were exceptions to the rule.

So you have to ask yourself: are the fees worth it? Realistically, they are probably not worth it in the long run. You have to go back to the argument that with an active portfolio, where you are going beyond market indexes, you are usually far better off buying something with the lowest cost, because costs will erode returns over time.

The famous founder of the index investing movement

at the retail level was John Boggle of the U.S.-based Vanguard Group. Boggle believed that all of the work put into investment strategy we have cited was critically important to his approach to investing. Benjamin Graham's *The Intelligent Investor* was Boggle's investment bible. In fact, Boggle admits that his worst mistake ever was ignoring the work of Benjamin Graham; that's when he fell into the trap of believing that indexes alone could work—until, of course, he found he was unable to outperform the markets over time. But, once again, there are always exceptions, and there are some portfolio managers who have been able to develop unique insights and do better than the vast majority of investors. You will tend to find these exceptional portfolio managers utilizing either the triple-A approach that we've been talking about or, perhaps, the portfolio strategy of investors like Warren Buffett and Charlie Munger, Buffett's co-manager of their portfolio. They have been able to consistently outperform over time.

The message of all of these landmark books on investment strategy is essentially the same: getting back to basics is the key to success. If you don't understand how a company operates, then you don't understand why you're buying that stock. You have to know how the company earns its money; where its profit comes from; its margin of safety; the reasons behind why it has real long-term value; how the owners or managers have built a moat around it, a defensible position that would be almost impossible to penetrate unless you expended huge amounts of money. Once you understand all you need to know about any given company before you invest in it, you can begin to build a portfolio of companies that have all of these elements in common. That is how you become a conservative, intelligent investor.

i. The issue of costs

The core goal for any investor, as we have said right from

the outset, is to have more money tomorrow than you have today. Unfortunately, most people don't fully grasp that proposition. In terms of back-to-basics investing, having more money tomorrow means dealing with the issue of costs today.

Costs matter. If you are a long-term investor, there can be no question that the erosion of capital through management expense ratios (MERs) can be quite significant over time. If your investment advisor or mutual fund manager is getting two-and-a-half or three percent of your money over a period of, say, 20 years, that's an awfully large chunk of your capital going out the door that would look a lot better in your hands.

Compare, for example, the performance of a portfolio where you've invested, say, $10,000 in an international equity fund over 10 years paying an MER of three percent, to a similar fund where the MER is 1.95 percent (which is sort of my plateau). Assuming the funds have almost identical returns over that time, there can be no question that the fund with the higher MER will result in much more lost profit potential over the 10-year period, and that profit potential is going straight to the fund advisor and to the fund company.

The truth is most fund companies can make extraordinary profits at fees under two percent. If you include their compliance costs, administrative costs, reporting costs, regulatory and filing fees, the portfolio manager's fees, and everything else, probably as much as 50 basis points drops to the bottom line. And that also includes a substantial amount for trailer fees paid to the financial advisor, which I don't object to as long as the base MER is within reason and some real value service or unique concept is being provided. The differential in these numbers is quite substantial in terms of long-term return, and the further you go out and the greater the return, the greater the actual capital loss.

Doug Lawson, a certified financial planner and certified management accountant, has conducted some very interesting research on long-term international equity funds with different MERs and reasonably similar returns. He found that the lost profit potential over a period of 20 years on an MER of 1.95 percent versus three percent is enormous. Incredibly, it amounts to over $50,000 in a portfolio of $150,000 with about a six percent average rate of return. The total fee differential is significant because these are dollars that could have been in your pocket.

And if we look at funds that performed even better, the lost profit potential gets even worse. On average, Lawson figures that about 20 to 25 percent of returns are lost over time on these long-term scenarios. That is all money that could have been yours—money that didn't have to be paid but you chose to give away because you didn't understand how critical MERs are when it comes to controlling costs.

Management expense ratios in Canada have not gone down the last few years. In fact, they have actually appreciated an average of about 20 percent per year. The mutual fund companies, meanwhile, are reporting record profits, which reinforces my argument that it is better to buy the companies that offer the mutual funds than the mutual funds themselves in most cases. The mutual fund companies are invariably more profitable and perform better than many of the investment products they offer. For this reason, a pure-value, low-cost equity portfolio built around the triple-A methodology is probably the most conservative and, probably, also the most effective investment strategy you could ever follow.

In addition, don't forget that things like MERs and other fees, charges, and costs also count with respect to things like income trusts. Canadians have stashed away $90-billion in these vehicles in their quest for cash flow. But think about how these offerings come out: the underwriting firm's going to get five percent right off the top; the salespeople get another five percent; plus, there are all sorts of other fees built into them. So the old "fund-of-funds" strategy just layers fees upon fees upon fees. But in some cases, that portfolio approach can mitigate some risk. And having 30 or 40 different diversified fund-of-fund concepts, in terms of an income trust in a portfolio, isn't such a horrible idea if that's where you want to be invested. I would prefer to buy it inside an insurance contract, where, once again, there is a higher fee, but it makes the total return tax-sheltered. That is critically important to us all.

John Boggle stresses that while a low expense ratio is the single most important factor in evaluating a fund, it is not the only one. Boggle also advises people to consider the fund manager's tenure on the job and the frequency of fund trading, or the turnover ratio. The turnover ratio in Canada is critically important because it determines the distribution factor in terms of tax liability sent to you in reporting slips at year-end, as the fund must disperse those out to the unit holders if it is held outside a registered investment. Portfolio turnover is also a critical component because, as the portfolio is turned, the brokerage firms are making all sorts of commissions along the way; turnover of more than 100 percent per year is certainly far too high.

So the lower the turnover, the greater the long-term tenure of the portfolio manager, the lower the MER, and the higher the quality of the stock within that portfolio, the greater potential there is for long-term return. When you integrate all these dimensions you have a much greater potential for making real money, and that's what this is supposed to be all about.

ii. Cash flow

Cash flow matters. The intent in investment strategy, especially as it relates to retirement planning, is to generate multiple streams of cash flow. You want to control the cash flow that you have, of course, but you also want to continue to generate multiple streams. I used to call that "multi-streaming," because the objective is not only to have diversified investment structure but also diversified investment cash flow so that you don't have to rely upon just one source. Plus, you want to manage the risk on it at the same time. By having multiple income streams, you are managing risk, you are managing cost, and you are managing tax concurrently, so it is a synergistic strategy.

If you are successful in creating multiple streams of cash flow that are tax-reduced, tax-deferred, or, in some cases, tax-free, you will avoid the claw-back taxes and higher tax brackets that normally befall well-financed seniors who are now in retirement and over the age of 65. Higher tax brackets are a particular problem for retirees because the current tax structure in Canada has placed the brackets so close together that, in many cases, the moment someone rolls to an RRIF they are bumped to a higher bracket.

When it comes to creating multiple income streams in today's low-interest environment, buying GICs may not be the best option. Recent studies conducted at York University have shown it is next to impossible for GICs to produce any return outside a tax-sheltered structure. This is nothing new, of course; for the last 30 years it has always been better to buy a GIC inside an insurance policy, where you can get bonus interest and it is sheltered from taxation.

Likewise, if you would prefer to buy an income trust, you can usually find a clone or derivative of most trusts available inside insurance products. A number of insurance companies have developed products derivative of certain mutual funds, funds-of-funds, and income trusts for the specific purpose of providing investors with a shelter from taxation. The cost for this service is about 50 basis points, but you're eliminating a whole level of tax. And by borrowing against the capital inside the insurance policy, you have created a tax-free cash flow called an insured pension plan structure. This cash flow, of course, is non-taxable because it is a borrowing. The money is repaid on the death of the taxpayer when the estate gets the benefit of the insurance contract, and the interest on the investment capital inside the universal life insurance policy accrues and is not charged until the individual passes on.

The back-to-back annuity is also a useful cash flow vehicle. It gives you a guaranteed cash flow, part of which is a remission of capital with minimal taxation, and, at the same time, a guarantee of capital on the passing of the owner of the annuity. The back-to-back annuity is an excellent strategy for someone over the age of 65 because they get an insured pension plan from the investment account inside their universal life insurance policy, plus they are working to shelter their money long-term by using a plan of systematic withdrawal. With a systematic withdrawal plan you are allowed to remove about eight percent of your capital tax-free for the first six years because, again, it is considered a return of capital rather than income.

Meanwhile, the income trusts inside the insurance policy are also a bundled incremental benefit and can be used as an insured pension plan that provides a very strong cash flow. Most of these cash flows are around six, seven, or eight percent annually in a guaranteed structure. We know how much we're going to get and how long we're going to get it, therefore we're not subject to market fluctuations. That's exactly what you need if you want to be in control of your cash.

iii. Keeping the cash you have

Being in control of your cash means developing multiple streams of cash flow, but it also means finding ways to save, control cash outlays, and recapture cash you thought you had lost. And while some of these capital conservation strategies may sound trivial, they can help investors of all ages to improve their financial position.

For example, paying down credit card balances to

eliminate non-deductible interest of 18 to 28 percent should be an absolute no-brainer when it comes to capital conservation strategies. The average household currently has about $8,250 in credit card debt, and the interest on that debt is costing families literally hundreds and hundreds of dollars a year, so there's no question this can be an enormous saving. And credit card debt is non-deductible debt, so once it is discharged we can then use that money for investment purposes.

Believe it or not, holding a garage sale to clean out the junk in the house once or twice a year is also good idea. The average house will have about 5,000 dollars' worth of clutter in it that's available as tax-free cash. Most people don't think of it, but there is a cost attached to storing this stuff and having it lying around. First of all, it takes up space, and second, it depreciates the value of your principal asset—your home. So why not take the cash you have invested in the useless junk in the garage, the basement, and the attic and use it to invest in something with real value or to discharge some of that non-deductible debt.

Also, with record gasoline prices and rising insurance costs becoming a permanent fact of life, weaning your family off of the idea of having multiple cars is also a good idea. Like it or not, public transit will save you money; studies show that it costs anywhere from $18 to $20 an hour to drive a car most days. You have the initial cost of the car, plus its depreciation, gas, insurance, maintenance, and other things like highway tolls and licence fees. All told, it costs somewhere in the neighbourhood of 40 cents a mile to operate a vehicle right now. If you absolutely must drive, then you need to manage those car expenses wherever possible, but if you can overcome the driving addiction altogether you can save a lot of cash.

You also might want to cut down on your bad habits. For example, being an abstainer can lead to significant insurance savings, not to mention save your life. If you drink less, smoke less, gamble less, and cut out other non-sensical expenditures, which are really voluntary forms of taxation, you are going to save money, have more invest-ment options, and, last but not least, improve your health. Remember, they're not called "sin" taxes for nothing. Rich people generally move away from smoking and certainly don't buy lottery tickets. Lottery tickets were actually cre-ated to distract the poor from their situation and to ensure that they stayed poor. Like cigarettes and booze, lottery tickets are not just bad cash management, they are anoth-er voluntary form of self-destruction.

Buying used and "second time around"-type items can also save you a fortune, and it's not hard to do in our recy-cling-oriented world. The average household spends about $1,850 dollars a year on clothing, but buying things at auctions, garage sales, clothing recycling stores, and on Internet sites such as eBay can cut into that amount sig-nificantly. Toys, sporting goods, and baby furniture are all prime garage sale merchandise, and buying some things there can cut your costs in half. Now this doesn't mean you have to turn into the kind of frugal individual who collects balls of string, but there's nothing wrong with saving a few dollars every chance you get. That's how rich people got rich in many cases. Frugality, discipline, living below your means—they're all excellent capital conservation strategies.

Interestingly, studies have also found that homebod-ies—people who like to stay at home and don't overspend by eating out too often—tend to have more money than individuals who eat in restaurants a lot. Statistics show that Canadians spend an average of about $1,800 annually on entertainment and about $2,100 on eating out. That's 3,900 after-tax dollars gone forever. Entertainment is clear-ly an important ingredient for a happy life, but there are ways to cut down how much you spend on entertainment and eating out without turning into a recluse. For exam-ple, doing things like borrowing books from the library instead of buying them, sharing videos and CDs with friends and relatives, and having family barbecues and dinner parties at home all offer good entertainment plus save you lots of money at the same time.

Cutting down on your household expenditures is also important when it comes to capital conservation. If you are lucky enough to have the space to rent out a room or a basement apartment in your home, and many seniors are in this position, you could earn yourself an extra $4,000 to $5,000 a year. Of course, you must select your guests carefully, making sure to get an honest and reliable tenant. In some cases it is even possible to negotiate a deal where the tenant helps out with ongoing home maintenance and chores like cutting the grass and shovelling snow, tasks that many seniors must pay to have performed. Basically, the bottom line with a large house is this: use it or lose it. It is going to cost you just as much for heat, light, air conditioning, taxes, and insurance in your big house whether you use all of it or just half of it. Therefore, if you have space that's not being used, rent it out. If you don't want to rent the excess space you are not using, sell the house, downsize it.

> On average, the rich save **22%** of their average income, versus **2.5%** saved by the general population.
>
> They do this through **frugality, discipline, planned spending,** and **avoidance of impulse purchases**.

When it comes to maximizing your cash flow so it provides you with the optimum benefit, it is essential that you use your living space efficiently. And, of course, in today's low-interest-rate environment you should cut your mortgage cost by staying variable. These savings are very significant because, once again, they involve after-tax dollars and just make common cash management sense.

There are also things you can do to save cash when it

comes to investing. First of all, you should consolidate all your brokerage and investment accounts in order to avoid the fees, especially the non-deductible fees. Remember, every transaction fee you don't pay is more money in your pocket. In terms of investment strategies, you should perhaps consider strategies you haven't looked at before. Don't be afraid to look at new ways to shelter money from taxation so you can create better cash flow. If you do proper tax planning at the beginning of the year, that is going to reduce the withholding tax when you file your T12/13s or your TD1's with your employer. Again, less withholding tax on every paycheque or reduced quarterly instalments means more money in your pocket. That means better cash flow, more money for investment, and more money to pay off non-deductible debt.

Here are a few more cash saving tips you may not have thought of:

- Did you know you can raise your car and house insurance deductibles and save on your insurance costs? Deductibles are usually reviewed every two years, and in today's high insurance-cost environment you could save as much as $500 a year by raising yours. Those are after-tax dollars right in your pocket.

- Review your long distance telephone carriers and shop carefully. There are lots of choices in the long distance marketplace today, some involving special dial-ups where you have to listen to a short advertisement and some available online. In some cases, it is possible to save as much as 50 to 60 percent a month on your long distance bill by switching carriers. Projected over a year, that could amount to several hundred dollars in after-tax money depending on your usage.

- Change your credit cards. Many credit card companies are now offering some cheaper rates, so it is not a bad idea to shop around. You should also try to consolidate all your credit card debt on one card. And when card companies offer you big rewards or cash rebates, it usually just means higher fees, so shop carefully and read the fine print.

- Review your Internet and wireless providers. Once again, you can often get the best rates by consolidating several services on one bill. Some companies offer significant bonuses and rebates if they provide all services.

- Replace the light bulbs in your house where possible with compact, high-efficiency fluorescent bulbs. Even though these bulbs cost five to seven dollars apiece, the energy cost to run high-efficiency bulbs is 30, 40, or even 50 percent less than the cost to run standard 100-watt bulbs. It might sound like a trivial thing, but this kind of careful utilization of cash inevitably leads to more bottom line cash flow dollars.

- If you are going to do any travelling, by all means book as much of your trip as possible online. Not to knock the wonderful people out there in the travel agency business who do excellent work in helping people make customized travel arrangements, but you can save as much as 50 percent on hotels, airfares, cruises, and rental cars by booking online. Naturally, you must read everything carefully and make sure you do proper research on the properties and places you are going before you book, but the savings are real.

- If you are buying any electronic equipment, especially computers, once again, the Internet may be your best place to shop. By researching brands and comparing costs in the comfort of your own home, you can avoid spending hundreds, even thousands, more than you want to when you actually enter the electronics store. And the more cash you save, the more cash you have.

There is no shame in watching carefully how you spend your money. In fact, rich people are often some of the cheapest people you will find; that's how they are able to afford so much luxury. The truth is the rich are just very good cash managers, keeping track of every penny and making sure it is being used to the best advantage. Some people might call that being miserly, but I call it an important element of proper financial planning.

PART 2

Exploding the Myths

i. The lessons of the past

Proper financial planning also involves taking a good hard look at some of the basic strategies that, over the years, have gradually turned into ingrained investment dogma. Dogma of any kind is usually never completely correct, and you should never be afraid to challenge its validity. Unfortunately, there just is not a lot of good empirical research being done in Canada, outside of the few exceptions we have mentioned, that challenges the prevailing beliefs that currently govern the investment world.

To begin with, how did the Baby Boomers lose their way? Right now, across North America, there are between 80 and 85 million Baby Boomers active in the investment marketplace. During the 1990s, so many of these individuals were investing heavily to build wealth for their retirement that the market entered a cycle of irrational exuberance that threw the old conventional wisdom about investing into the garbage can. "Get rich quick" was the new dogma; everyone started chasing short-term performance and the advice of hot fund, top fund, best fund. Investors would frantically buy investment products with no intrinsic long-term value that promised nonsensical returns of 80 and 90 percent. Common sense and restraint were pushed aside as outmoded ideas, so much so, in fact, that in 1999 the major financial media called Mr. Buffett and his buy-and-hold approach to investing "irrelevant." Then, of course, the bubble burst.

How could it happen? Investors have been told over and over again for years that past performance is not a predictor of future returns, yet many people chased past returns during the boom. Most investors know to avoid risk to capital at all costs, yet many people ignored even the basic elements of risk during the boom. People also forgot that the companies selling the stocks and the funds were making money no matter what happened. They got the mine and you got the shaft, as the old cliché goes, and Bre-X is the perfect example.

In a very interesting book called *Bull! A History of the Boom of 1982–1999*, published by Harper Business Press, author Maggie Mahar exposes the ignorance and avarice that created that great market bubble and eventually brought it crashing down. Essentially, Mahar blames the whole mess on a rare confluence of naïve investors, greedy career fund managers, and an irresponsible mass media joining together to promote the same irrational ideas. That confluence sparked a buying frenzy that swept up both naïve investors and the ones who should have known better. The process was also aided by relaxed securities commissions and major strategic errors by the Federal Reserve. The noise created by these combined factors succeeded in drowning out the voice of conventional wisdom.

Many Boomers lost their way because they were driven by greed and ignorance during the heady days of the "new economy" boom, but not every investor got burned when the bubble burst. There were a few conservative investors, Mr. Buffett chief among them, who remembered how money was actually made and protected their capital during that time by only going after stocks that fit the old Benjamin Graham model.

This is not to say, however, that the "buy-and-hold" investors were not trading stocks during the boom; even a value investor will abandon the buy-and-hold concept if a particular stock no longer meets the required criteria. Value investors always try to buy stocks for the long term, but they know there is always an appropriate time to dispose of a stock that has lost its value.

The Boomers who lost their shirts did so primarily because, blinded by greed and ignorance, they bought hype instead of value. When the hype evaporated and the illusion of value came crashing down, the net result was the loss of 30 to 40 percent of retirement assets. For the average investor, the implications of that loss are that they will have to work five to seven years longer to recoup that capital. Freedom 55—forget about it.

On the bright side, we can only hope that the experience of the tech bubble has shattered three dangerous illusions forever: that analysts provide any value; that audits can be trusted; and that management is always acting in the best interest of the investor.

ii. What is a realistic return?

Jonathan Clemens, writing recently in his very useful weekly column in the *Wall Street Journal*, stated a harsh truth: most of our investments won't make money over time, even in the long term. According to Clemens' research, after the negative influences of tax and inflation are factored in, most stocks generate returns of only about two percent a year, and have done so since about 1950. That means the notion of a given stock producing returns of eight or ten percent is simply not realistic, and many investors spend an awful lot of time chasing utter nonsense. If you want to know how much return you really get from a given stock, you must first factor in inflation, transaction costs, and taxes. What's left is the real return.

This holds true with all investment products. With bonds, for example, the results are barely ahead of inflation, and with money market funds the returns are zero or negative. Clemens' research shows that most individuals, through active trading, through the lack of understanding of value, through the generation of taxation, through the costs of transactions, and after inflation, simply do not appreciate their capital over time. Instead they transfer their wealth into the hands of governments and financial institutions.

Realistically, in a properly structured portfolio, if you can make six percent after tax, inflation, and transaction costs, you're probably doing pretty darn well. If you can make eight percent, you're doing extraordinarily well. In our studies of what the rich do, we found that most high-net-worth individuals only look to be in that six-to-eight percent area. They don't look for the big home run, as many of the Boomers did during the tech bubble. So, clearly, unless you can come to terms with what your returns should be realistically, it is more than likely you will end up making no money on your investments.

iii. The diversification myth

Another pearl of bogus wisdom peddled by the financial planning industry is the notion that investors must spread their investment dollars around various markets and sectors in order to avoid isolated downturns and achieve sustained growth. In fact, if you have ever talked about investing with the financial advisor at your local bank you will know that they seem to chant the word like a mantra—"diversify, diversify, diversify."

The rationale behind the diversification strategy seems logical enough; it's just too bad it doesn't work. A study of nearly 1,800 actively managed domestic stock funds from 1984 to 2000 found that the less diversified funds actually had higher returns over time. Conversely, the portfolios that were highly diversified and actively traded did not outperform over time. The results of this study, which was conducted by a group of academics at the University of Michigan, were discussed by Mark Hulbert in a column in the *New York Times* (Hulbert is also the editor of the *Hulbert Financial Digest* and a regular reporter on CBS and a syndicated radio show).

Given these findings, it is probably safe to assume that the performance of Berkshire Hathaway stock may have more than a little to do with Mr. Buffett's belief that diversification is not always a good thing. "If you are a 'know-something' investor," wrote Buffett in a 1993 letter to shareholders, "spreading your bets among a large number of stocks is likely to hurt your results and increase your risk."

The Berkshire Hathaway structure is clearly not consistent with a widely diversified portfolio. The company's stock has not been riskier than the overall stock market as judged by the volatility of its returns. In fact, since 1965, when Mr. Buffett took over the management of Berkshire Hathaway, the yearly percentage change in the company's book value, one barometer of Mr. Buffett's investment ability, has been 16 percent less volatile than those of the S&P 500 index. Despite that, Berkshire has outperformed the index 34 of the last 39 years and performed nearly 12 percentage points a year above the market index.

However, there are academics and financial professionals who look upon the performance of Berkshire Hathaway as an exception. The conventional wisdom is that the less-diversified portfolios will be, on average, significantly riskier than the more-diversified ones, and therefore will not perform better. Of course, this is not true. The research clearly shows us quite the opposite: among managed, industry-concentrated mutual funds the researchers found the more diversified the structure, the less the return. Conversely, for funds more focussed in concentration, the results were far better.

Interestingly, this finding holds true even when investing in small caps. Researcher Jim Gore, who works with O'Donnell Mutual Funds and the new O'Donnell Small Cap portfolio, studied this very issue and found that he could only focus in on 10 small cap stocks at a given time. Why? Gore says the inherent risk and high volatility of small caps basically put him into a situation where he needed to monitor every stock very closely, but once he got beyond about 10 or 12 stocks, he couldn't do the job adequately. The triple-A portfolio model essentially says 10 blue-chip stocks are about as far as anyone needs to go because of the nature of what is in that portfolio. So if you are determined to be in small caps, a concentrated, focussed, undiversified small cap portfolio will probably do dramatically better than a highly diversified one, regardless of what the financial advisor at the bank says.

iv. The asset allocation myth

According to long-held conventional wisdom, asset allocation, or how we divide our money among equities, bonds, and cash, will determine the vast majority of the potential performance return. This concept first took hold back in 1986 with the publication of the article "Determinants of Portfolio Performance" in the *Financial Analysts Journal.*

To be precise, this famous study, which has been cited perpetually by the mutual fund industry, said that 90 percent of the return came from asset allocation and only 10 percent from stock picking. If you believe this to be true, then it logically follows that stock pickers, and therefore active managers, provide no value. On the other hand, in light of the period we have just gone through where, as reported by Levi Folk in the Fund Library, there was no difference between bonds or stocks in actual performance, asset allocation also appears to make little if any difference when it comes to explaining returns. So what really does have the most influence on portfolio performance? Is it asset allocation, stock picking—or neither one?

In fact, what that 1986 study essentially said, and subsequent studies have reiterated, was that the overall performance of a given portfolio has more to do with the volatility of return, its fluctuation up and down, and the collection of pension funds, than it has with asset allocation or stock picking. Basically, performance has nothing whatsoever to do with the actions of individuals and it has nothing whatsoever to do with absolute and real returns. It has very little to do with risk for that matter as well. It is the volatility, the fluctuation of returns over time, that ultimately determines overall portfolio performance.

So how important is asset allocation really? In truth, not very, but it's an interesting idea.

v. The active trading myth

Think you can beat the bear market? Well, the research says very few people can. A study recently reported, once again, by Mark Hulbert in *The New York Times*, showed that about 20 percent of frequent traders significantly outperformed the market. Now, while it is interesting that 20 percent of frequent traders analyzed in the study succeeded, it is even more significant, it could be argued, that 10 percent of frequent traders did abysmally badly and 70 percent trailed the market when transaction costs were included. It is also interesting to note that the same study found that if you compare female active traders to male active traders, the women, who generally trade less often, did better than the men.

The bottom-line finding of this study, it would seem, is that the vast majority of active traders rarely outperform over time. That means as many as 70 percent of the investors out there are likely much worse stock pickers than they think they are and they might be better off either taking that triple-A approach or moving toward index or exchange traded fund strategies. There will always be a few successful day traders or active traders who do very well selecting stocks, but this research clearly shows that very few of them will outperform over long periods of time. Of course, this study only looked at a period of about seven years, so whether or not the active trading approach works better over, say, a 25-year period remains to be seen.

vi. The price/earnings myth

Another popular misconception that has taken hold in the

financial planning marketplace is the price/earnings myth. There is, apparently, no linkage of market price/earnings multiples to subsequent returns, no matter how you measure the ratio and no matter how long a period of time you actually look at in terms of measuring returns. If you are looking for evidence to back up this position, a series of articles published in the *Journal of Portfolio Management* clearly exposed the lack of linkage between price/earnings multiples and subsequent returns. Those articles encourage investors to gravitate toward cash from operations divided by the stock price as a better indicative measure, rather than earnings divided by the stock price. Companies that have relied totally on price/earnings multiples to estimate their returns are more than likely in for a big disappointment because, once again, quite the opposite is probably true. Unfortunately, the research that is emerging suggests that a big chunk of the price/earnings-based information currently in the marketplace is little more than random guessing.

vii. The myth of mitigating risk

That brings us to the elements of risk. Many investors today turn to brokers and financial advisors to retool their investment structures to mitigate risk. Unfortunately, most of the complex risk gauges currently used by money managers are essentially worthless.

Most risk-mitigation tools are based solely on theory. Risk measurement is typically equated with price volatility and is employed by money managers to select stocks, but guess what: the results usually don't make the real return worth it. Financial advisors commonly use and misuse risk measures such as beta, which calculates the tendency, or lack thereof, of a stock or portfolio of stocks to exaggerate the market moves. So in a week when the market is up six percent and a given stock has a .5 beta, that stock is likely to gain only three percent. Contrary to the popular notions, beta is not a measure of volatility. A high-volatility gold stock could have a very low beta. In theory, high beta stocks are supposed to be riskier but provide higher returns, while low beta stocks provide less risk and lower returns. However, this theory rarely works in practice.

It is interesting to note that a classic 1992 paper by Professors Eugene Fama and Ken French (Fama and French are essential reading for all financial analysts) demonstrated convincingly that there was no correlation between beta and return. High beta stocks or portfolios have provided lower returns and vice versa. Therefore, as we like to say in the industry, "beta schmeta."

Similarly, many advisors like to trot out a risk-mitigating strategy called the "information ratio," a strategy in which you divide a portfolio's excess returns above the S&P index by its volatility. But not only is this benchmark flawed, it flat out doesn't work. Many companies like to use these basic measures to determine risk, but risk is not something that can be measured by these traditional benchmarks, and using these risk measurement tools will not give you any additional margin of safety and protection of stock price. What you will generate is mostly fallacy that has no long-term validity in the marketplace.

In addition, investors should know that value stocks and value mutual funds lose their lustre in outperforming growth funds over time after fees, transaction costs, and the over-diversification of portfolios are factored in. An empirical study conducted jointly by the University of Chicago and Dartmouth College and headed, once again, by Fama and French, showed that if transaction costs were not taken into account, value stocks have indeed significantly outperformed growth stocks in the last 76 years. However, if you place value stocks and growth stocks into separate mutual fund portfolios and look at their returns, the funds produce similar results when expenses and diversification are factored in.

viii. Exploding the myths

Much of the current misinformation making the rounds in the financial planning industry got its start during the speculative binge of the 1990s. Like any other binge, that one produced a veritable cornucopia of investment fallacies. In retrospect, many of the ideas about investing that came out of that time were patently absurd, like the idea that we could all quit working and basically make a living being online and day traders, or the belief that you could get an accurate idea of a company's results from their financial statements. And then there was the one about projections being an accurate predictor of future earnings.

That last theory might work as an investment strategy if you also believed that stocks were the best investment for the long term. Unfortunately, most investors, especially during the 1990s, were simply not willing to wait a long enough period of time—let's say 20 years or thereabouts—in order to test the theory. Ironically, there is reasonable evidence to support the argument that stocks probably will beat bonds and cash over the long term. This, of course, is supposed to happen because corporate earnings are all but certain to grow faster than the economy and the price/earning multiples will rise as a result.

A corollary to this is the notion that market dips are really opportunities to buy, not warnings to get out. This theory, however, certainly won't work in the sober investment years ahead any more than it did in the last few years. Unfortunately, when we look at the long term, profits on average can't grow faster than the economy. In a democracy, capital share of the economy's pie can't keep growing while labour shrinks. So what can we expect from the economy? Well, if the GDP is going to average two or three percent, don't expect that the stock yield will grow that much stronger, especially with price inflation and everything else taken into account. It may be as high as three or four percent, but still not jaw-dropping. Long-term treasury returns have also averaged somewhere in that range.

So if we look at recent history, is it likely that stocks will always outperform over time? Once again, it is a difficult thing to predict with certainty because investing is not a precise science. If we look at a factor like stock price appreciation, for example, anything over five percent actually begins to lose its appeal when we consider the inherent market risk. Just remember: if you lose 50 percent of your investment on a stock, you must then make 100 percent on it just to get your money back. That is as good a reason as any to start moving away from this cult of equities and the great stock fallacy that has dominated our thinking for the last decade or so.

Of course, the so-called experts will continue to claim they can create a risk-adjusted return in your portfolio through proper asset allocation, but now you should know better. Regardless of what the financial planning industry says, you know that investing is not a precise science. In fact, it's probably not a science at all. You also know that strategies like asset allocation probably don't even work over time. In truth, the most important lesson to learn when it comes to personal finance is that most of the strategies in this industry are, at best, hit-and-miss, and that most of the clichés repeated over and over by the investment "experts" are not supported by any kind of substantive research.

Conclusion

i. The intelligent investor

What is the difference between the intelligent investor and the run-of-the-mill investor? Well, the intelligent investor looks at all the elements involved in the investment process: fees, taxes, transaction costs within the portfolio, active trading, creating a margin of safety. They look at the cash from operations and try to determine value without following many of the traditional measures. Most of the nonsense we hear coming from the financial planning community is just noise and hype that does nothing to reduce risk, and the people who make their investments based on that noise and hype will generally find that they don't make any meaningful returns.

Intelligent investors have done their homework using the available research, so they know how to separate investment myth from reality. They know that GICs outside of structured tax-sheltered vehicles don't work; that growth and value stocks produce identical returns because of active trading; that beta is not a measure of risk; that the price/earning multiple is valueless over time; that you can't really outperform markets over time; and that the stock equity structure is not the only methodology.

Given all of these facts, it should be apparent now that a proper investment structure includes those blue-chip equities, looks for dividends and cash flow from a number of sources, mitigates risk, and maximizes the tax efficiency of the portfolio. The truth is we don't need a lot of stuff; the intelligent investor gains power over their financial future by simplifying the process. The financial planning industry, meanwhile, works to take that power away from you through meaningless jargon and terminology and ineffective structures and clichés that create confusion and increase ignorance. In fact, the whole cult of equities was built around that noise and confusion. Their power comes from the nonsense, and you lose power when you buy into it.

ii. The X-Factor approach

We want you to be a successful, intelligent investor, and the way to be a successful intelligent investor is to take the holistic approach that integrates everything into one comprehensive plan. That means you need an investment plan, a tax plan, a cash management plan, a retirement plan, and an estate plan. You need to integrate these plans into one comprehensive package because they are interrelated, the results are synergistic, the costs will come down, and it will put you back into control of your financial future.

The X-Factor approach to investing says you will be far more successful than most people in the marketplace today if you do a few critical things. First, you must control the risk you take on by protecting capital at all costs, because costs clearly matter. Second, you must try to take control of the cash flow you generate, because cash flow is critical for retirement. Finally, you must do everything you can to reduce the amount of tax you pay. If you do these three things successfully, you will gain control over most other factors in the marketplace.

Can financial advisors play a role in this process? Yes, if they are holistic financial planners; if they put you in control of your own financial future and don't lead you down the well-worn path of diversification, asset allocation, or one of the other elements of nonsense we've talked about. More often than not, it is the unstated goal of the financial advisor to take control of your financial future because they work for a specific fund company as a tied seller of their in-house products. Obviously, someone offering insurance from one company is not going to do the same job as someone who is independent and can shop the market to cut your costs, to give you more investment options, and to get you a higher credit rating from the insurance product providers. The same thing applies in terms of investment strategy. The individual who is a holistic investment strategist, who helps you manage your portfolio around the X-Factors, is more likely to put you in control by focussing on cost reduction.

This does not mean, however, that "fee for service" financial planning is always a bad strategy. In most cases, though, that initial fee should be the only fee you end up paying. Remember, if you are spending more than 1.95 to two percent on transaction costs, management expense ratios, and other things like that, unless there's an enormous strategic investment or tax advantage, it's just not worth it. If you find that transaction costs and fees are eroding the bulk of your investment return, it's time to re-educate yourself and start asking your investment advisor some tough questions, because it's your money not theirs. And if your advisor tries to answer those tough questions by bringing up things like "diversification," and "asset allocation," you can tell them to stop right there. An intelligent investor knows that holistic financial planning is really about structuring the portfolio for maximum benefit with regard to risk, cash flow, tax, and costs. When you can successfully integrate those factors, you have an X-Factor portfolio.

What we've tried to do with the X-Factors is to formulate and apply exceptional investment and financial planning strategies appropriate to the extraordinary times we live in. The research shows that we must challenge the conventional wisdom that currently rules the marketplace. As more and more investors near retirement, we must take control of our financial future. Times have clearly changed. Taxes have gone up, not down. Asset structures have declined, and the big returns of the past are no longer there. Most investment products pushed by the financial planning industry have not made you wealthier, they have made you poorer. Financial institutions have merged, meaning there are now fewer options in the marketplace. In a world of multiple investment products, few product providers, and governments that have most of us in a gigantic tax trap, if you do not control the controllables, you surrender any potential for long-term financial security.

If you are trying to determine the best way to take control of your financial future, you might ask yourself: Would Warren Buffett invest my money in the same way I do? Would Benjamin Graham invest it the same way? Based on what they have written and their actions over several decades of investing, it is fair to say that both Warren Buffett and Benjamin Graham would be X-Factor investors. John Boggle would be an X-Factor investor. Clearly, when we look at the marketplace as it exists today, only the X-Factor strategy works for the long term. Why? Because it is rational, it is simple, it is tax efficient, it is cost efficient, it generates good cash flow and, more important, it protects capital by cutting your overall risk.

By taking the X-Factor approach to investing and personal finance you essentially do what the rich do: rich people want to stay rich; they want to protect their capital; they want to be tax efficient; they want to limit their costs; they want to have cash flow to maintain the lifestyle that they want. If you can't grasp that, then you are very likely doomed to play the part of an observer in your own financial destruction. You won't be alone though—that's what most people are doing; they are getting poorer, not richer, with each passing day because they don't understand that these are extraordinary times, and exceptional strategies are required to deal with them. So abandon the clichés and put yourself in control. If you do, you will succeed—and that's what X-Factor investing is all about.